DOWNRIVER —
A Memoir of Choate Island

Agnes Choate at twenty.

DOWNRIVER—
A Memoir of Choate Island

BY MARY AND ROGER CHOATE WONSON

POEMS BY AGNES CHOATE WONSON

PHOTOGRAPHY BY ROGER CHOATE WONSON

FOREWORD BY MARTHA WONSON BRANDT

ESSEX RIVER PRESS
BEVERLY, MA

ACKNOWLEDGMENTS

In gratitude to all who helped make this book possible, especially to Mrs. Francis Fuller, Barbara Lindo, and Dana Story for sharing old pictures from their photograph collections; Barbara Risley, who listened and shared the ups and downs; Martha and Bob, who saw mistakes we didn't; Arthur Francis for boat trips to Choate Island; our family for patience and encouragement; Choates of the past who kept diaries and journals; and Mom, who believed we could do it.

A big thank you to Peggy Roell and Paul Theriault, volunteers for the Trustees, who faithfully reproduced the second edition to help keep the memories alive. Also, thanks to Tom Beddall who painstakingly reviewed several drafts of the second edition and helped fine tune it.

FIRST EDITION

Copyright@1983
By Mary and Roger Choate Wonson
Beverly, Mass. 01915

SECOND EDITION

Copyright@2024
By Roger Choate Wonson
Beverly, Mass. 01915
ISBN 978-0-9992959-1-5

All rights reserved. No part of this book may be reproduced in any form without written permission of the copyright owners, except by a reviewer who may quote brief passages in a review.

PRINTED IN THE UNITED STATES OF AMERICA

To Agnes

who helped us begin

and whose spirit inspired us to finish

our tribute to her memory.

FOREWORD

Dear Reader:

I am writing as the youngest of the three daughters of Mary Sue and Roger Wonson, who are the author and photographer of this book published in 1983. How our family has grown and changed in the 40 years since then! Now there are 8 adult grandchildren and 9 great grandchildren of Mary Sue and Roger.

Sadly, our sister DeeDee, Mary Sue and Roger's second daughter, died in 2013 of brain cancer, a heartbreaking loss for all of us. In 2022, our mother Mary Sue Littlejohn Wonson, an incredible cook and writer, died at age 100. Until a few months before her death she remained her zesty and creative self, even publishing an article in the Boston Globe a month before her 100th birthday! Today our father, Roger Choate Wonson, is 100 and still enthusiastically playing saxophone and drums for family and friends. We feel so blessed.

Please enjoy the following poem I wrote during one of our many family trips to Choate Island. Poetry has often been a part of a Choate Island excursion. I participate in the annual Trustees of Reservations sponsored Choate Island Day to read aloud poems by our grandmother, Agnes Choate Wonson (1882-1981) who was the last Choate to grow up on the island. Her love and creativity inspire us still.

Martha Wonson Brandt
Spring 2024

Choate family reunion - 2012.
Left to right: 4th row standing 3rd person, Dee Dee Wonson Stearns; 3rd row sitting 1st person, Mary Sue Littlejohn Wonson; 3rd row sitting 3rd person, Roger Choate Wonson; 3rd row kneeling 5th person in row, Kathy Wonson Eddy. Right to left: 4th row standing 2nd person, Martha Wonson Brandt.

Cherished Choate Island

I have been to an island
Cherished by those
Who have walked these
Scraggy knolls
Long ago
Yesterday
A myriad of times

The stones themselves
Worn smooth
Polished by many
Determined steps

Today we pilgrimage
To the homestead atop
The burnished grassy knoll
We represent many
England, Germany
A whole lifetime of
Choate

The house whispers to us
Sun streaming through
Pale colored glass
Reflects its soul
Upon the stair

Floor boards creak and bend
Wistfully underneath
The weight of many
Laughing, boisterous
New Choate children

The house sighs
An ancient urge
Of remembrance and
Peace

We gather there
Fulfilling the promise
Living and loving
Carrying on the generational
Destiny of a life
Well lived
Where hope and love
Abound

Our unity is our strength
We leave this island today
To once again return
A nuance of grace
Accompanies our departure

Wraps us in
A tapestry of
Sea salt marsh and the
Sweet breathing of the flowers
Tenderly we grasp
The hands closest to us
Pass on this energy
Of island history and truth
Embody its cherished ancestry

Cultivate a lasting
Love of our heritage
Where nothing dies
Or leaves this place
A constant renewal
Faith
Hope
Love

Martha Wonson Brandt

CONTENTS

INTRODUCTION — xiii
A nostalgic day on Choate Island.

THE ISLAND — 17
The geological and geographical background; Agawam Indians, first settlers; natural beauty of a sanctuary for wild life and flowers.

CHOATES OF HOG ISLAND — 25
Direct lineage from John Choate, owner in 1678, to Agnes Choate; new insight through family journals, diaries, and records.

THE CHOATE HOUSE — 35
A tour of the plain, yet functional, Choate homestead; descriptions and stories of the rooms and old attic.

THE ROAD, FERRY, & BRIDGE — 47
An informative and often humorous account of the building of a road, ferry and bridge connecting Choate and Dean's Islands, from a diary written by Rufus Choate in 1880.

SUPERSTITIONS, TALES & WITCHCRAFT — 57
Accounts taken from family diaries, old newspapers and Essex County records.

NEW-MOWN HAY — 63
Agnes' memories of haying time and farm life on the island.

A SUMMER PLAYGROUND — 69
Childhood experiences; the social life of the island's summer guests, a time of games, parties, and music.

EPILOGUE — 81
A farewell.

BIBLIOGRAPHY — 83

INTRODUCTION

Return to an Island

Past orange-bronze marshes I went today
    To an island I used to know.
The sea gulls circled and curved above
    As they did in those years ago.

Tide was at flood, and the channels ran
    Gray-green and silver-blue,
A West wind piled up marching clouds
    Just as it used to do.

The lonely brown farmhouse on the knoll
    Seemed waiting for me to come
While it sunned itself on the slope of field
    'Midst the chorus of crickets' hum.

It was good to stand on the worn, flat stone
    By the heavy-beamed oaken door,
And I felt the homestead was glad, indeed
    To welcome its child once more!

Agnes Choate Wonson

Until her death in July, 1981, Agnes Choate Wonson was the only living member of the last Choate family to own and live on Choate Island. It was her family who sold the island in 1916, ending almost 250 years of Choate ownership.

Born in 1882, she summered on this island in the Essex River, Essex,

Massachusetts, for thirty-one years. Through her poetry, writings and story telling, she has preserved the island's haunting past and absorbing beauty. Any visit to the island with her was a memorable event, but especially we recall a beautiful day in the early 1970's when all of us in her family made a special nostalgic trip downriver.

There was excitement at the Essex wharf as passengers boarded and we loaded lunch baskets, thermoses, cameras and extra jackets. Slowly we made our way past the restaurants lining the causeway, the smell of fried clams permeating the atmosphere. We rounded the bend past Clay Point, white with discarded clam shells, then Bacon's point with its cluster of summer cottages. At the open entrance of salt marshes, we had that indescribable first smell of salt air from the ocean. Cautiously following channel markers, we twisted and turned on the sun-sparkled meandering river, one moment the wind in our faces, the next at our backs. Before us loomed the familiar long, hog-shaped island mound, one end dark with trees and the other an open grassy slope where the weathered brown homestead rested on the knoll, serene and silent, framed by blue sky. Deer dotted the rise; and just as Agnes described in her poem, sea gulls circled and curved in the sky where white clouds puffed and rolled. At high tide the orange-bronze marshes gave the appearance of a large wind-swept lake with patches of ruffled water. At the edge, the ribbon of white sand dunes resembled snow out of season, their whiteness intensified by the deep blue of limitless ocean.

As we gazed at the unspoiled beauty, our silence was broken only by water lapping the side of our anchored boat, rocking us gently. Shallow water covered the beach, which was deep with clam shells left by the Agawam Indians, the island's first inhabitants. We pushed and pulled our way up the thick bush bank to the open expanse of the slope, the ocean breeze swishing the tall grass around our feet.

As we climbed the rise toward the house, Agnes' face revealed her joy of returning to her summer playground. She began to describe the island as it used to be. On the right in the fringe of basswood trees was piano rock where she and her sister played house; to the left the long barn filled with sweet new-mown hay; standing in a row the guest cottages dubbed *Bungalow, Barnacle, Binnacle* and *Barber Pole*; the main house with its broad porch and picket fence always painted white when she lived there; the worn flat stone at the side door, the old well framed by two giant elms; parties, music, haying time…

During our picnic lunch in front of the old house, Agnes shared family stories and tales of seven generations of the Choate family who had owned the island. When we toured the house, each room seemed vibrantly alive through her memories released as fragrances from an old chest. Later we took the winding road to Hill Field, the large grassy summit of the island. The path led us through a grove of pine trees, silent except for branches soft-brushed by the whispering wind and a haunting hum of island insects. From the top of the hill, the air was so clear the blue domes of Mt. Agamenticus in Maine rose into view. The ragged line of sand dunes gave the appearance of snow drifts heaped high. We remembered that on this hog-shaped island's summit, the Agawam Indians established their lookout fort in view of their sacred burying ground. Here, too, in this quiet and beautiful spot is the grave of Cornelius Crane, son of Richard Crane who purchased the island from Agnes' family in 1916.

As we rested on the grassy knoll, Agnes continued to tell her stories of island days. Through her we saw and felt the island's past and sensed the eternity of its future. Here on this island had been a deliberate life rhythm, an intense love and closeness of family. The islanders were self-sufficient in an atmosphere of comfort, peace and security.

It was on this day as we shared Agnes' happy memories of Choate Island that the idea for this book was born. As her daughter-in-law, I felt an urgent compulsion, a mission to help keep the wealth of her memories alive for the generations to come. I have written, not as an historian with recorded data, nor a geologist to discuss the island's glacial formation, not as an architect to argue the construction date of the old house. It is my wish, through the memories of Agnes to be a part of the survival of the historical past, a time and way of rural life when men and women helped shape the future with their visions.

Agnes Choate Wonson's poems reflect the peace and security of her Choate Island days. They are intimate and revealing, portraying with simplicity and charm the strength that comes from a rich heritage. In her long life, Agnes made many transitions with grace and acceptance through her ability to preserve the past in her poetry and writings. Through my childhood memories of life in the deep South and Agnes' of her island, we shared a comparable love of the past, of a simple rural life. It is through this kinship of souls that Choate Island has become significant to me. It is a wealth of happy memories and knowledge of life that my husband, Agnes' son, and I want to share through old diaries, journals, family records and her poems.

With deep appreciation for Agnes—mother, poet, artist, musician and friend—we offer this book, her memories from the heart. May they be as enduring as the marshes and limitless sea surrounding the island she loved.

MARY AND ROGER CHOATE WONSON

Beverly, Massachusetts
April, 1983

THE ISLAND

In Essex River, Essex, Massachusetts, lies Choate Island, a mound of land resembling the back of a large hog, rising 170 feet above sea level. Commanding a sweeping panoramic view of dunes, salt marshes, blue water and the mainland, the gentle waters of Castle Neck River and Hog Island Channel lapping its shores, it is a place of history, folklore, natural beauty and a wild-life haven.

Physically, the island is a drumlin, glacier-formed, covering over 135 acres with a rocky, abrupt landscape on the Northern side, a gentle slope to the water's edge on the East and South. The lawyer, Rufus Choate who was born on Choate Island in 1799, lovingly described the scene as "sculpturesque, its beauty consisting in clearness and grace of outline, in boldness of relief and in its setting of untarnished blue."

Choate Island, the largest, seems nestled in a grouping of smaller islands; three of these were important to Agnes during the years she lived on Choate Island. It was to Corn Island she went to dig clay for molding animals and flowers, to Dean's Island where her father helped build the bridge and ferry, and to Dilly Island Agnes made annual trips with her father to gather salt hay. Other islands, some gravel, some drumlins, are Bull, Round, Long and Great Bank. At low tide the islands appear to be trying to rejoin by the connecting marshes and mud flats.

The first inhabitants of Choate Island were members of the Agawam Indian tribe who owned it until 1638 when it was sold for 20 pounds to John Winthrop of Chebacco, now known as Ipswich, Massachusetts. Members of the Choate family owned the land from the time John Choate began purchasing common lots in 1667 until 1916 when it was sold to a representative of Richard Crane.

The island was presented to the Trustees of Reservations in 1974 by Mrs. Cornelius Crane and is now open to the public. It is a unique sanctuary with very few unscheduled intrusions, reached by boat only at high tide after a meandering, cautious trip down the Essex River.

In 1650 a law was passed to forbid felling trees on the island. Later, however, cutting timber for fuel and building construction was allowed, diminishing the

The hog-shaped mound of Choate Island rises from the waters of Essex River. The Choate house is in the clearing at right.

wooded areas until the island was almost treeless. After Mr. Richard Crane purchased the island, many seedlings were planted and today it is a haven for wild life and birds. According to literature provided by the Trustees of Reservations, it is a sanctuary for deer, opossum, raccoon, otter, skunk, fox, muskrat and mink in their natural habitats. I remember on the day our family walked up the hill to the summit, a mother fox was alerted by our approach and cleverly feigned a broken leg to lead us away from her young. Deer darted gracefully in and out of the trees as we climbed the path.

In the shallow waters may be found green heron, blackbacks, sandpipers, black-crowned night heron, herring gulls and blue heron. On Castle Neck are terns and piping plover. In the swamp thickets during spring migration there are warblers, thrushes, blue-gray gnat catchers and fly catchers. The sand dunes provide protection in the winter for the snow bunting, sparrow and mice searched for by hawks hovering above. Enjoying the island as a sanctuary, it is difficult to identify with a journal notation of 1873 when Mr. Channel, an Essex resident, described an account of a duck shooting. "From a boat, a man shot twice into what seemed acres of ducks and geese and picked up twenty-eight he had killed."

From Hill Field, the highest point on the island, Masconnomet, Chief of the Agawams, could gaze at the beauty and wonder of land owned by his tribe. It was from this vantage point he could have a magnificent panoramic view of gleaming rivers, hills, groves, winding streams and broad ocean stretching eastward where sea and sky seemed to meet. Even though the Agawams' possessions in Massachusetts reached from the Merrimac River on the North to Salem and Manchester on the South, from the ocean on the East to Andover on the West, it was on Choate Island the chief chose to spend his summers fishing, digging clams, farming and gathering sweet grasses for basket weaving. Nearby, there were quantities of salmon, other native fish, clam flats and game from Jeffries Neck. Even during the years Agnes lived on Choate Island, the beaches were several feet deep with clam and oyster shells left by the Indians. Bones of deer, auk and other creatures were uncovered when the fields were plowed. Fish played an important part in the diet and culture of the Agawams, the name being interpreted "A Fishing Station, Fish Curing Place or Ground Overflowed by Water."

As early as 1608, Captain Harlow landed in the Chebacco area on a voyage in the interest of an English Company; and after Captain John Smith anchored in the bay, he wrote the following description in his *History of Virginia*:

> The people of Angoan used Captain Harlow's men kindly. This place might content a right curious judgement...On the East is an Isle of two or three leagues in length; the one half plaine Marish ground, fit for pasture or salt ponds with many faire high groves of mulberry trees and gardens. There is also Okes, Pines, Walnuts and other woods to make this place an excellent habitation...

However, it wasn't for the love of the scenic beauty or the availability of fish that the chief of the Agawams chose to live there. The hill could be used as an excellent lookout post for warrior duty to report the yearly invasions of the dreaded Tarrantines from Kennebec and Penobscot, Maine, who crept silently up the shore in their long war canoes. There were two forts in the island area; one across from Castle Hill and one on Choate Island. The fort on the island was built of earth and rocks and was thirty feet in diameter. As late as 1890 traces of it could be found. The island provided a grand lookout so strategically located that, from its site, all approaches of danger from the sea could be seen and signals sent to nearly all the Indians in the Chebacco area.

The Agawam tents were made from bark of trees or skins of animals, perhaps spread over a frame of strong poles in a circle then brought together at the top leaving a hole for smoke to escape. Piles of clam shells surrounded the wigwams. These were called "kitchen middens."

Chief Masconnomet and his tribe summered on the island until successive battle losses and the plague of 1617 gradually reduced his number of warriors to fifty. Finally, in 1638 the island was sold. No descendants of the Agawam tribe are known to be alive.

Even in the early 1900's when Agnes lived on the island, members of Indian tribes made yearly pilgrimages to the area, picking scented sweet grass on Dilly Island to make baskets. Once when she was a little girl, she and her sister were playing near the well on Choate Island when some Indians approached asking for a drink of water. She remembers her father eagerly questioning them about their ancestors and Indian stories passed down from other generations.

On a small island near the western side of Choate Island is an Indian burying ground belonging to the Agawam tribe. At high tide it is covered by water; at low tide, many relics have been found. Agnes describes this area: "Among the marshes to the West of the Island is a small patch of island-land, pebbly and stony. Here some of the island Agawams were buried. Often covered at highest tides, it is quite hard to find. My father knew just where to look. We treasure greatly the many fine arrow-heads, stone sinkers and a fine tomahawk head."

Agnes visited the burying ground many times, since it was a major point of interest when visitors came to the island. She described its isolation, a place sacred to the Agawams.

The Indian Burying Ground

A lonely little mound of stones
    Stands there amid the still high tide.
The river, with its loving arms
    Around it circles, deep and wide.

White sand dunes guard it from the sea
    This bit of land where Indians rest,
While quiet solitude of marsh
    Encloses it on south and west.

The mists of years have rolled away
    And from the rocky shores of Maine
There floats a fleet of birch canoes—
    The Tarrantines are come again!

The lookout on the hillside's brow,
    Where island fort of rocks lifts high,
Sees dusky paddlers slipping swift
    To mouth of river coming nigh.

                      Agnes Choate Wonson

Hauling lumber to Choate Island on the frozen Essex River.

Even though Agnes lived on the island only during the summer months, she was captivated by the biting winds, the foaming ocean and hushed beauty of winter. Often the water of the Essex River froze deep enough to allow cars to be driven downriver to the island. These trips inspired Agnes to describe its winter beauty.

Island in Winter

Winter is leaving white footprints
    On meadow and marshland and hill
And I think of an island down river
    That is snow-swept, lonely and still.

No pathway winds up from the bass woods
    To the homestead half-hid, drifted high.
There is only a white frozen silence.
    There is nothing but snow-waste and sky.

Then gray wings weep over the upland
    And there echoes a seagull's cry!

Agnes Choate Wonson

Looking across the bay from Choate Island, the white sand dunes appear to be great snowdrifts forming an outdoor theater, their ripple-marked designs and shapes varying with the seasons. In the winter, they reminded Agnes of great gray cats.

Winter Dunes

Like great gray cats asleep, dunes lie …
    Their rusty grasses like whiskers grow.
Among their paws curled lazily
    Gray-silver tide waves ebb and flow.

Gray sand, gray sea, gray pewter sky;
    Gray frosted shells left on the shore.
Cheerless, the dunes in winter lie
    Waiting for summer-time once more!

Agnes Choate Wonson

The marshes surrounding Choate Island are ever-changing with the seasons, ever beautiful. They become nature's carpet of colorful sea lavender, goldenrod and silver weed in late summer and fall, furry white in winter, soft pastels in spring. Young spring blades of grass crunch underfoot, their sparkle resembling clusters of brilliant diamonds. Charles Townsend in *Sand Dunes and Salt Marshes* describes the scene as "one with ribbons of water wandering like veins through the marshes reflecting the brilliant blue of the skies. The tall thatch bends before the wind, and shimmering waves, like those on the surface of water, pass over it." Robert Crowell, author of *History of the Town of Essex* described a trip to the island noting that the "sun gladdened all the salt meadows; the birds, secure in their hidden sanctuary of bushes and tall grasses, carolled their approval."

One never tires of the restful, quiet beauty of the changing landscape. The character of marshes and dunes is as enduring as the island heritage itself.

The Marshes

Have you seen the waste of salt marsh
    When the fog has left its haze
On the winding, blue-gray river?
    Have you seen it on such days?

Oh, the sweep of sun-burnt orange
    Oh, the bronze-gold stretch of brown!
Purple hills with steeples pointing,
    In the distance lies the town.

And the sunny silence settles
    Where the still creek channels flow
For September marshes beckon
    And my soul and I must go!

                  Agnes Choate Wonson

Geodetic map of Hog Island, known locally as Choate Island.

CHOATES OF HOG ISLAND

It is little wonder that because of its unique shape the island was called Hog Island for approximately 250 years. However, the time came when the residents of Essex decided to re-christen the island by the name of Choate. An account of this ceremony in the *Essex County Mercury*, October 20, 1887 reads: "It was on a lovely October day in 1887 when the brilliancy of the foliage and the beauty of the scene were surpassingly fine and inspiring, that there was an imaginary gathering of the descendants of the so-called 'Governor Choate', proprietor and first settler on the island in 1690 and it was unanimously voted and declared with the consent of the present owners that this island so romantic and sacred in family history and association, should thereafter be named and known as Choate Island; and it was so entered, by order of the selectman, upon the town records." Even though today many refer to it as Choate, legally the name was never changed. On geodetic maps and in records it is called Hog Island.

During the period when members of the Choate family lived on the island, there were eighty Choates born there; the first, a daughter of Thomas in 1691; the last, Rufus Choate the lawyer in 1799. Among them were ministers, lawyers, military captains, magistrates, members of the Governor's Council, representatives to the General Court of Massachusetts, state senators, one U.S. senator and one judge of Court of Common Pleas and Probate Court.

In spite of their deep love for the island and their appreciation of its beauty, no Choate was buried on it. The only graves are those in the Indian burying ground, those of twin daughters of the slave, Ned, and that of Cornelius Crane at the top of Hill Field, a site facing the coast of Maine which he loved.

In discussion of the Choates who lived on the island, only the lineal descendants (indicated by an * in the following genealogy) will be discussed in detail. Those starred include John Choate, the first Choate to own land on the island, his son, Thomas Choate, the first Choate settler on the island and Agnes Choate, member of the last Choate family to own it.

THE CHOATE ARMS.

John Choate—baptised in Groton, Boxford, Colchester England, 1624; d. 1695

    John, b. 1661; d. 1733
    Margaret, (n.d. of birth); d. 1692
    Samuel, (n.d. of birth); d. 1713
    Mary, b. 1666; d. before 1691
    *Thomas, b. 1671; d. 1745
    Sarah, (n.d. of birth and death)
    Joseph, b. 1678; (n.d. of death)
    Benjamin, b. 1680; d. 1753

*Thomas Choate—b. 1671; m. Mary Varney, 1690; m. Mrs. Mary Calef, 1734; m. Mrs. Hannah Burnham, 1743; d. 1745

    Anne, b. 1691; d. 1759
    Thomas, b. 1693; d. 1774
    Mary, b: 1695; d. 1767
    John, b. 1697; d. 1765
    Abigail, b. 1699; n.d. of death
    *Francis, b. 1701; d. 1777
    Rachel, b. 1703; d. 1783
    Ebenezer, b. 1706; d. 1766
    Sarah, b. 1708; n.d. of death

*Francis Choate—b. 1701; m. Hannah Perkins, 1727; d. 1777

    Francis, b. 1728; d. 1740
    *William, b: 1730; d. 1785
    Abraham, b. 1732; d. 1800
    Isaac, b. 1734; d. 1813
    Jacob, bapt. 1735; d. young
    John, b. 1737; d. 1791
    Hannah, b. 1739; d. 1785
    Francis, b. 1743; d. young

*William Choate—b. 1730; m. Mary Giddings, 1756; d. 1785

    William, b. 1756; d. 1756
    *David, b. 1757; d. 1808
    William, b. 1759; d. 1835
    George, b. 1762; d. 1826
    Margaret, b. 1764; n.d. of death
    Job, b. 1766; d. 1813
    Mary, b. 1767; d. 1852
    Hannah, b. 1770; d. 1810
    Sarah, b. 1772; d. 1801
    Lydia, b. 1774; d. 1839

*David Choate—b. 1757; m. Mary Cogswell, 1784; m. Miriam Foster, 1791; d. 1808

    Mary, b. 1792; d. 1855
    Hannah, b. 1794; d. 1837
    *David, b. 1796; d. 1872
    Rufus, b. 1799; d. 1859
    Washington, b.1803; d. 1822
    Job, b. 1806; d. 1808

*David Choate—b. 1796; m. Elizabeth Wade, 1828; d. 1872

    David, b. 1828; d, 1918
    Helen Maria, b. 1831; d. 1851
    *Rufus, b. 1834; d. 1913
    Hannah, b. 1840; d, 1910
    William Cowper, b. 1843: d. 1918
    Washington, b. 1846; d. 1918

Rufus and Sarah Burnham Choate, last of the Choate family to own the island.

*Rufus Choate—b. 1834; m. Sarah Burnham, 1880; d. 1913

    *Agnes May, b. 1882; d. 1981
    Celia Mason, b. 1884; d. 1976

*Agnes May Choate—b. 1882; m. Arthur Stanley Wonson, 1916; d. 1981

    Arthur Stanley Wonson, Jr., b. 1918; d. 1993
    Roger Choate Wonson, b. 1924

As early as 1561 the Choate family was known as Van Choate and lived in the Netherlands. When a decree of death was issued by Phillip II of Spain against Protestant Dutch inhabitants who refused to conform to edicts of the church of Rome, some Choates found refuge in Essex and Suffolk Counties in England; others sailed to New England, accepting the customs of the new country and dropping Van from their name. At the age of 19, John Choate, a pioneer settler in the new country, came from England in 1643 and purchased land for a homestead in what is now Essex, Massachusetts. Choate Island was held as common land by the town of

Chebacco, or Ipswich, until it was divided into lots of 3, 4 ½, and 6 acres each and made available to citizens. In 1667, John Choate began buying shares and by 1690 owned almost a third of the island lots two miles away in full view from where he lived on the mainland. In 1678 he purchased the portion of land on which the first island Choate home was built.

John was a good business man, high spirited and energetic. It was said of his escapades that "he was a hard case and no one but a clergyman could handle him." He enjoyed any association with the courts, either as a witness in cases for others (such as Rachel Clinton who was charged with being a witch) or as a result of his own misdeeds of stealing apples and the like. "His wits and brains were largely exercised in getting himself out of his law scrapes and he seems to have stamped his personality upon his descendants to such a degree that large numbers of them have taken to the law as naturally as ducks to water." Perhaps in an effort to make amends, he stated in his will, "I bequeath my soul to God."

John Choate's land was given to each of his sons (except the youngest, Benjamin, for whom he provided a college education). Thomas received the Hog Island property. Only 19 when he married, Thomas and his young bride were the first Choate settlers to live on the island. It was a pioneer life, difficult and hard; but he possessed many natural talents and proved himself a great farmer. His house was located a few rods behind the existing Choate house on the island.

During the thirty-five years that Thomas lived on the island he was known as "The Governor" because of his supremacy as a prominent landowner and his qualities of leadership. Referred to as a "spruce young man" and because of his strong mind and quick perception, he was an influential power in town and public affairs. An interesting story of Thomas when a young boy is recorded in a family record. Once when a guest visited the family, Thomas met him with no shoes on. "You are barefooted, I see," the visitor greeted him. Thomas quickly replied, "Yes, Sir. I was born so."

Thomas served in the General Court for four years. He was well informed with a strong determination and the ability to express himself clearly and precisely on any subject. Because of his qualities of leadership and warm friendship with the Rev. John Wise, his minister, he signed a letter and supported the unsuccessful efforts to free his own wife's uncle, John Proctor, who was condemned to hang as a witch. Even though all who signed ran the risk of being executed themselves for their sympathetic actions, he witnessed John Proctor's will three days before he was executed.

When Thomas moved off the island to the mainland in 1725 he owned so much property in the town and on the island that it was written of him: "The Governor is a good man but evidently trying to carry too much of this world's goods." However, in 1727 he was so disturbed by an earthquake that in one day he gave three farms away to his three sons, the south farm on the island going to his son, Francis, who lived there with his young bride, Hannah.

The earthquake, which occurred soon after Francis and his bride moved to the island, profoundly affected many people living in the parish and caused his own spiritual reawakening. It was noted by a local historian that "on the Sabbath Day at night, about ten of ye old clock there was a great earthquake throughout the Province which shook the houses and threw down the tops of chimneys in many places. It so affected the minds of people, that it was a means used by the Holy Spirit to produce a very powerful revival of religion in the Ipswich parishes." Prior to this renewal of religious interest, Francis had reprimanded his slave, Ned, for leaving the island frequently to attend religious meetings but after his own conversion confessed that he didn't wonder why Ned loved going so. Later he was considered a tower of strength in the fervent religious Whitefield Movement.

"Esquire Francis," as he was called, was good to his slave, Ned, his wife, 'Binah, and their large family. When only eighteen years old, Ned had been given to Francis by his father, Thomas, who bought him in Boston upon arrival from Africa. 'Binah (Sabina) was obtained by Francis after he moved to the island. Ned and 'Binah remained on the island until their deaths, preferring to do so even though Francis provided in his will for their freedom if they chose it. The will provided also for their comfortable support when old and unable to work. Francis moved to the mainland in 1738, leaving Ned on the island to care for the house until Francis' two sons and their brides came to the island to live in 1756. Ned lived to be 90 years old. An amusing story was recorded in a family journal about Ned when he was an old man. "When a daughter was born to David Choate in 1792, Ned was vexed she was not a boy; and when her sister arrived in 1794, Ned was again disappointed. He said, 'Mr. David's wife's no fool—she'll look out for herself first.' "

Even though he was not a seafaring man, Francis was interested in all aspects of maritime life. With his brother Lt. Thomas Choate, he built three bankers of about 60 tons each called *Dove, Neptune* and *Swan*, using hand-sawed lumber from trees on the island and doing the blacksmith work himself. The *Dove* and *Swan* were seaworthy for 70 years. It is believed that the point of rocks on the western side of Cross Island which juts out into the river was the location of the fish house, wharf and fish flakes owned and operated by Francis.

Francis was interested in political affairs and kept in close touch with any news of the Revolutionary War. It is said that as he was dying, his close friend, the Rev. John Cleveland "jumped on his horse and flew to his bedside saying, 'Burgoyne has surrendered!' The dying man waved his hand with patriotic joy lighting up his face but was too far gone to speak."

When Francis died in 1777, he left the island farm to his son, William. Even though his parents fitted him for college, and wanted him to become a minister, William

Lawyer and orator Rufus Choate, last Choate born on the island.

rejected the whole idea and instead became a master in the science of navigation, a knowledge he passed on to his four sons. At the age of 25, William became captain of a ship and later owned several vessels. During the winter he sailed to southern ports and farmed on the island in summers. In his journals and diaries, everything was regulated by tides. One son's birth was listed as "high water," another at "low water in ye morning."

William had a thorough knowledge of mathematics and at one time wrote a book listing rules and problems for geometry, trigonometry and navigation, in which he excelled. He established a school and taught on the island, the students ciphering on birchbark. His own children were provided with great educational opportunities, being better educated than most families on the mainland. It was his custom on Sunday evenings to have the family gather, one child reading aloud. Each was required in the daily routine to be in the process of reading a book.

Incidents are recorded of William's wife, Mary Giddings, showing her bravery, quick thinking and courage. During the Revolutionary War, men were stationed on the island to prevent the landing of British vessels. When the boats were approaching, all on the island fled except Mary, who declared she would stay with her two children. She remained and was unharmed. At another time, Mary Giddings acted quickly, saving her daughter's life. William wrote a letter to his son, David, who was in the army, describing the lightning storm on the island:

> "...I would inform you by this letter that through the goodness of God we are all pretty well...On the 12th of August we had some thunder before sunrise with small showers of rain, and about eight a.m. the house was struck with lightning. There was much damage, six of us being in the backroom, one in the chamber and four in the garret. We were all much stunned, and Lydia, who was in the garret was brought down as dead but soon revived by her mother and was pretty well by the next morning. Such a remarkable dispensation of God's power and goodness I hope we shall never forget but be prepared for death at all times. It is thought by such as have seen the house a remarkable interposition of Divine Providence that no lives were lost..."

This incident resulted in the conversion of another daughter but had little influence in changing William's non-church member status in spite of his father's lifelong wishes.

David, who inherited the island farm from William, was never very well and spent many years traveling to improve his health. At one time his doctor had suggested a trip to Spain, but he became ill after everything was loaded on the boat and had to return to the island farm. He kept a detailed diary beginning at age 21 describing his trips, noting his marriage date, the tragic loss of his first wife, life on the island and his experiences of marches, deaths, hunger and victories in the Continental Army. In the *History of Essex*, David was described as "a man of uncommon intellectual endowments. To a quick and accurate perception, a ready and full recollection, he added a judgment ever ready to decide, and was never under the necessity of making more than one decision on the same subject. From childhood, books were among his dearest companions, and though denied the advantages of a regular education, he arrived at a degree of improvement often unattained by men of the present opportunities and possessed talents which would have been an honor to a statesman. In the social circle, none were his superiors. The learned found instruction and amusement in his company and the ignorant went away satisfied that they were persons of information because they had been conversing easily on subjects before unknown to them. His friendship was firm and unabating. The man who possessed his confidence had a safe deposit for the most important facts."

David was interested in the country's political welfare, writing influential letters and articles. One appeared in a Boston newspaper in favor of ratification of the Federal Constitution in Massachusetts with the signature "Farmer." It is recorded that when the historian, Dr. Sewell, was to go to Chebacco, he was told to "be sure to see Mr. David Choate on the island as he is the only man there is." David died when his son, Rufus, the well-known orator was only 9 years old. His wife, Mariam Foster, lived to know their son's success.

In David's will, the island property was left to his son, David. Even though he had a limited formal education, David was a man of rare intellectual gifts with an insatiable thirst for knowledge and enthusiasm for study. At 19 he became a teacher and because of his intense interest in education was instrumental in inaugurating and developing the high school idea in education, founding the Essex County Teachers Association, serving as trustee for Dummer Academy in Byfield, Massachusetts, and a member and chairman of the Committee on Education in the State Legislature. He used illustrative apparatus in teaching and his keen interest often extended beyond the classroom. Frequently he took his pupils out at night to survey the heavens, teaching them to name the stars and trace the course of planets in orbit. He emphasized the wisdom and majesty of a creator who could control the starry heavens. He belonged to a group of seven men who acted as pioneer advisors to Miss Mary Lyon in establishing Mt. Holyoke Female Seminary in 1836 and served as a trustee for eight years.

In addition to his educational interests, he served for several years as Justice of the Peace. He had an active interest in agricultural affairs. In the Essex County Agricultural Society he was vice-president and trustee and in 1860 made a survey, writing nearly 100 pages entitled *An Agricultural and Geological Survey of Essex County*. He was a statesman, serving in both branches of the State Legislature. His interest in local affairs helped promote the branch railroad. His writings were never dull or obscure, often humorous. He kept detailed statistical records of all activities in which he participated.

Even as a boy, David had a passionate love for music. He was a skillful performer of many instruments, including the bass viol and flute, taught singing schools and for nearly fifty years led the church choir. He was an active participant in his town's civil, educational and moral welfare. In his church he served as deacon for almost fifty years and Superintendent of Sunday School for nearly thirty-five. Indeed, his great-grandfather Francis would have been proud of him for his calm and dignified inspiration toward higher ideals and better living. He had a strong conviction that "Life is God's choicest gift to man and it lies within the power of each one of us to make of it what he will. If it is of any value at all it is worth living in a manner acceptable to Him who gave it."

David showed great oratorical qualities, a gift shared with his brother, Rufus, the advocate. He could adapt himself to any occasion and audience with an insight into grasping the subject and researching material, presenting it with wit and enthusiasm. As a public speaker he was animated, sympathetic and sometimes eloquent.

David's son, Rufus, inherited the island home. He had the same appreciation of the beauty and nature of the island and enjoyed farming during the summers he lived there. After attending Kimball Union and Dummer Academy, Rufus began the study of medicine at Dartmouth. It was discovered that he had non-corrective poor eyesight and could not continue his studies. Rather than being disappointed, he became involved in farming, outdoor life, town affairs and church offices. He, too, was active in public life, holding town offices and serving as church deacon. He was responsible for the Rufus Choate School in Essex. He had a deep love for the island home, its rich legacy and ancestral associations. He never tired of the unchanging outlook of the land and waters around him and was quick to perceive inspirations the island offered. He kept diaries, illustrating them with clever drawings. He inherited his father's love for music. When employed as a tuner by the Mason and Hamlin Organ Co. in Boston, he had the opportunity to purchase parts of an old organ in an old Boston church. Using these, he built and played an organ which he installed in the island home. Also, he served as church organist in Essex Congregational Church. He was intensely interested in church and town history, patiently hand copying the records.

His daughter, Agnes, was born in Essex, Massachusetts, attended Salem Normal School and studied art at the Eric Pape School in Boston. She taught art in Montpelier, Vermont for ten years and in the Essex school for twenty-five years after her marriage to A. Stanley Wonson. Even as a young girl, she began to write and draw for magazines and received payment of $1.00 for her first published poem at the age of 16. At 69 she won a trip to London in a limerick contest sponsored by the *Boston Post* and producers of the movie, *Enchantment*. Until her death in July, 1981 (approaching her 99th birthday) she was actively involved in submitting material for publication, reading, solving word puzzles and playing her Hammond organ in the nursing home where she resided. Her published works consist of poetry and craft articles for children, accompanied by her artwork. She was an excellent musician, inheriting her natural talent and love for music from her grandfather, David, and her father, Rufus. After her marriage in 1916, she lived in Essex until Stanley's death in 1975. There are two sons; Arthur Stanley, Jr. of Stuart, Florida and Roger Choate of Beverly, Massachusetts. There are five grandchildren and ten "great grands" as she affectionately labeled them.

Agnes transmitted a mood to the reader with ease through her poetry which portrays what she saw, felt and heard. Her writings are like an album to open at any time to feast again on the joys of earlier days. Through her love and appreciation of Choate Island presented in her creative works, she will live for the generations to follow who will be caught up in the island's lasting beauty and history.

THE CHOATE HOUSE

Standing serene in an idyllic unspoiled spot on the island knoll is the Choate house. Its isolation and severe simplicity reflect wise and loving care of a rural farming and fishing community of the colonial past. In early days the house served not only as home for members of the Choate family but as a district school and Sabbath meeting place for religious services.

There has been some controversy about the date when the Choate house was built. Most authors writing about Choate Island state that Francis Choate built the house in 1725. Presumably it was constructed two years before he and his bride, Hannah Perkins, moved there in 1727. His father, Thomas, lived in the first house on the island which was a few rods behind the present one. He moved to the mainland in 1725, legally signing over the island property to his son, Francis, after the frightening experience of an earthquake in 1727. The original Choate house was torn down about 1780.

Francis and his family returned to the mainland in 1738 leaving Ned, the slave, living in Francis' home. According to family records, Ned "carried on," taking care of the home until 1756, when two sons of Francis (William and Isaac) and their brides moved to the island. If the construction date of the present Choate house is as late as 1740 as suggested by some historical specialists, then it is assumed that Francis and Hannah lived with his brother and family who remained on the island in the original house built by Thomas. To say the least, this would have made a crowded household since nine children were born on the island between 1727 and 1738; six to Francis and Hannah and three to Thomas, Jr. and Elizabeth.

Also, it seems feasible that David Choate, grandson of Francis, would pass on any knowledge he had about the house to his son-in-law who wrote a book about Essex and the island. The Rev. Robert Crowell married David's daughter, Hannah, and visited the island many times. Since David was twenty years old when his grandfather, Francis, died, it is logical that he remembered direct family information and facts to give his son-in-law. Crowell wrote that the house was built in 1725. Also, David's son, Rufus Choate the lawyer, had a great love of the island where he was born and in his personal recollections states that the house was constructed in

1725.

However, more important than the exact date the Choate house was built is the fact that today it stands as a symbol of a way of life in which the Choate family made significant contributions to America's historical past. To appreciate it for that reason rather than get lost in search of factual knowledge is sensible and rewarding.

I Once Lived in an Old, Old House

I once lived in an old, old house; it stood
    Content and calm on gentle rise of hill
Its dim-paned windows peering from its hood
    Of tangled grapevine rambling there at will.

It faced southeast, this house of years ago,
    While through the plain square rooms thin sunlight played.
Two ancient elms with rustled whisperings low
    Stood guard above it with their tender shade.

I know the old house loved the distant sea,
    The river, chattering past the slope of shore.
Such hosts of memories, heart-dear to me
    Bring back those happy homestead days once more.

Old house, when twilight's lonely hour is there
    Perchance the dusk wind makes old shadows sway,
Makes shades flit slowly up and down the stair,
    The secrets of an old house, who can say?

                         Agnes Choate Wonson

Choate house restored. According to family records, the house was built about 1725 by Francis Choate, son of Thomas, the first Choate settler on the island.

On the day of our boat trip to the island, as we climbed the knoll toward the old home place, Agnes pointed out the original location of the 90-foot barn and the summer cottages standing in a row when her family lived on the island. Two giant elms by the old well seemed to protect the house. Agnes remembered that when she lived there the house was painted white and had a wide porch across the front. A white picket fence sloped down hill. Rising from the center of the roof as if anchoring the square rooms around it was a large chimney with fireplaces opening into each room.

As we crossed the large stone slab at the side door which led to the sink room, Agnes spoke of an incident that happened at this doorway when she was a little girl. "My family stayed on the island later that fall and I particularly remember playing on the floor in a patch of sun coming through the screenless space of the wide open door. Father's big white horse walked right across the slab into the sink room where I was sitting in the sun."

THE CHOATE HOUSE

Agnes explained that the sink room was so called because the wide wooden bench-like slab off the wall was used to hold sink pans, wash basins and buckets of water. A roller towel hung nearby. Large timbers were used for the corner posts and rafters. Still visible on one of the posts was a jagged gash made by lightning. "Mother said the shock, as the bolt struck, knocked her to the floor," Agnes recalled.

On one wall in the sink room the original wide paneled doors remained; one opened to the stairs leading to the second floor bedrooms and the other to stairs leading down cellar.

Predominant in the kitchen located next to the sink room was the large wall fireplace with dutch ovens. The small room on the eastern side of the kitchen was called the milk room because stairs led to a cool rock-lined storage space for dairy products. "This was our means of refrigeration," explained Agnes. "Mother kept milk fresh and cool in wide shallow pottery pans, skimming it frequently for cream to make butter."

The two spacious front rooms seemed flooded with light through window panes in pastel shades of amber, purple and gray. Noticeable were the wide unpainted floor boards, high studs and simple finish. On the fireplace wall in the east parlor room there was a corner closet with gracefully carved scalloped edges used to display china. It was in this room that Sunday night hymn sings were held with Agnes' father playing the melodeon or the pipe organ which he built.

The west front room was used as the dining or family sitting room. The same wainscoting surrounded the large fireplace, a similar plain wooden mantle over the fireplace. It was in this room Agnes remembered many happy evenings spent sitting by the fire listening to stories of the island told by her father. "Father had a special rocking chair in which he sat always, even pulling it to the table at mealtime."

From the front windows we looked out at the old well nestled between the two giant elms, the gentle hill slope leading to the blue water below.

The heaving H-hinged front door opened into a small hallway connecting the two front rooms. It is interesting to note that the angled stairway leading to the second floor has square newel posts and wide, molded edge planks instead of the traditional balusters. No paint was used on the woodwork throughout the house until about 1840.

On the second floor, we saw the high-studded front room known as the Rufus Choate room. It was here the lawyer and orator was born in 1799, the last Choate to be born on the island. Many Choate descendants have been rocked in the original Rufus Choate cradle, including Agnes' grandchildren.

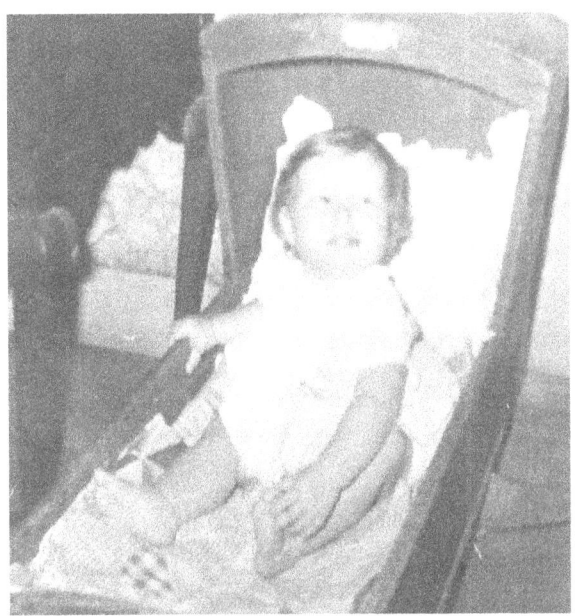

Agnes' granddaughter, Martha Wonson, rocked in the Rufus Choate cradle.

An Old Cradle

In shadowed attic of my mother's house
    Through many dusty, cobwebbed years has stood,
For I recall it even as a child,
    A quaint and time-worn cradle, formed of wood.
Its brown-stained sides rubbed bare by touch of hands,
    Long-vanished mother hands of a past year.
Inside its high hood's flare oft nestled snug
    Some tiny sleeping face, so soft, so dear.

Sometimes I almost think old furniture
    Remembers in a strange and silent way
Its other life…I feel it has a soul
    That guards so jealously its long-gone day.
I wonder if a saddened yearning comes
    While dreams the cradle of those years well spent?
Perchance, having fulfilled its destiny
    There, in my mother's house, it sleeps content!

                        Agnes Choate Wonson

Original raised panel wainscoting surrounds the fireplaces in the four front rooms.

"Our homestead was famous in its way as the birthplace of my great-uncle Rufus Choate," Agnes began a story. "In my childhood, parties often pilgrimaged to our island to see the room where the great lawyer was born. The big four-poster bed and the brown stained cradle in which he was rocked were of much interest. I remember a lady visitor once gave me a quarter after I had told her that the famous man was my ancestor. After that, I was not allowed to personally conduct sightseers until I was old enough to know more about my forebears."

During the years Agnes lived on the island, a crudely constructed wooden box was used in the kitchen for firewood. Many years after the island was sold, Agnes discovered that this "wood box" which she had stored in her attic was actually a Pilgrim period chest from the original Choate family bedroom furniture.

An Old Room

(In which my great uncle Rufus Choate was born)

I watch the orange sunset fade to green
Where hill-topped pines in silhouette are seen.
I love the brief, pale twilight of a winter day,
That gentle pause the light and dark between.

For oft the dusk brings memories to me,
An old room in an old homestead I see.
And in this southeast chamber, tall and high,
A fluted, four-post bed there used to be.

Across the room an oaken chest stood near
Brought from an old England in a former year.
My great-grandmother wove her linens white
And in this chest she laid them fine and sheer.

A brown stained cradle worn by time was there
I fancy many a mother's whispered prayer
Was breathed above a fuzzy-downy head
As slumber soothed she rocked with loving care.

A wide hearth warmed this room oak-beamed and low,
Along the wall stood ladder-backs, a row,
Rich is my life, to hold throughout the years
Such precious memories of long ago.

Agnes Choate Wonson

As often as his schedule as a Boston lawyer would allow, Rufus Choate returned to the sanctuary of the island, one of his homes as long he lived. From the windows in this upstairs room he enjoyed the panoramic view of the ocean, dunes, surrounding islands and marshes. In his memoirs, he described it as a "slope in front, a thick matted sward always green which runs down fifteen or twenty rods to the broken bank of the creek. There is a fringe of basswood and other native trees along the shore. The near view is of marshes at low water, with a tidal stream winding and broadening down to the bay. At high water all that field is as a quiet lake. The

Choate House, view from hill.

island's shelter from the sea is afforded by two bare arms of sand. The whiteness of the sand and the rounded heaps into which it is drifted by the winds, deceive the unaccustomed eye with the appearance of snow. Between the two points there is left an open space through which one looks out upon the limitless sea."

Little wonder he declared, "I'd rather be governor of Choate Island than governor of Massachusetts. "Besides," he added, "I like the chowder made from Ipswich clams more than all the edible French dishes of the Parker House bill of fare!"

Back of the Rufus Choate bedroom was one of Agnes' favorite rooms. "How I loved the little library and study on the second floor!" Agnes pointed out as we continued our tour. "A member of Great-Uncle Rufus' family sent my father a large shipment of books and magazines. Shelves were filled to the ceiling and we were allowed to color the pictures. We never minded rainy days." Agnes and her sister were fascinated with the discovery of an unusual small door on the back wall and asked their father to tell them its story.

"Long years ago," he began, "my great-great-grandfather, Francis Choate kept slaves. The little door you girls found today was actually the door opening into a covered passage-way which led across into the wood shed chamber where one of the slaves slept. Each night after his day's work, Ned would crawl through the small space to go to bed. Ned was very musical, a natural player of the bass viol. Often at night he crooned hymn tunes as he drew the long bow across the deep, mellow strings. He had two attractive daughters, Jane and Violet. It is sad to remember that during a corn husking in the barn one cold autumn night, they both caught cold and later died. Their graves are up in the far corner of Perkins' field on the island where you little girls go for wild strawberries.

"In the earthquake of 1727, Ned was terribly frightened. About ten o'clock on a cold, frosty night in October, a great noise, like the roaring of a chimney on fire, was heard. Shortly the shock began and lasted a full minute. Chimneys tottered and fell, and the earth burst open in several places. Great cartloads of dirt were thrown out. After the incident, Ned became very devout, influencing his owner, Francis, to attend church. A severe winter followed the earthquake, the snow so deep that there was no moving about except on snowshoes. Even the horses had to wear them!"

The original wooden latch opened the door to the stairs leading from the second floor to the attic. Most of the bedroom doors had hand-forged H hinges and crudely carved knobs. Whittled pegs remained in the closets. The heavy hand-hewn timbers held together with wooden spikes were amazingly preserved against salt air and strong winds. As we stepped into the large, lofty attic, the central plastered chimney dotted with signatures seemed to dominate the unpartitioned area.

Agnes and her sister often pretended they were members of the Agawam tribe, the attic their fort lookout.

The attic was a land of magic filled with old trunks, clothes, books, furniture, toys and dolls," Agnes described. "We never tired of our inventive games and play-acting. One rainy day when the northeast gale howled outside, and gusts of rain dashed across the roof, Sister and I were playing under the dusty eaves. The case of an old Queen Anne piano, the first in town, was a great attraction to us and we loved to thumb over its silent, yellowed keys. Other treasures were all about us; decoy wooden ducks, so life-like as to seem real; black stocking dolls; old trunks filled with musty garments. A high long-legged desk by the windows always interested us, with its yellowed documents of faded ink, scraps of old newspapers and letters of pre-Civil War days.

"One particular day, Sister had found scraps of velvet and silk in the trunks and was fashioning hoods and capes for her dolls. I was exploring the desk when I chanced to find a little cubbyhole I had overlooked before. Tucked away behind some yellowed scraps was a tiny partition with a little knob. I pulled, and a small drawer moved out. Quite excited, I explored this space. I remember thinking if this had been in a story plot, I should have found something wonderful—a will, perhaps, or some money, or a secret love letter. Alas, the only contents was a torn scrap of an old newspaper clipping."

The Old Attic

Tonight against my window beats the rain
    A southeast blow. It brings a picture rare.
    Once more a child, I climbed the attic stair,
Heard the wild gale, and watched the storm again.

How dimly seen, through driving mist, the shore,
    Wet waste of dunes, and out across the bar
    Gray lines of breakers flinging spoondrifts far
And through it all the sullen ocean's roar.

The attic! How we loved the dusty cheer!
    Among the cobwebs in one corner lay
    A quaint Queen Anne piano, once they say
Brought from old England in an earlier year.

A great square chimney in the center stood
    On which with glee we wrote our names each year,
    Under the eaves, such treasures would appear
Black stocking dolls, decoy ducks made of wood.

And constantly the patter of the rain
    Made ceaseless din on shingled roof o'erhead,
    It rains tonight; but how the years have fled.
Would I come play those attic games again!

                    Agnes Choate Wonson

From the windows in the attic, we had a sweeping view of ocean and dunes and could see the winding road path leading to the summit of the island.

"How I loved climbing that road," Agnes reflected.

Original latch on door in sink room of the Choate house.

Front hall stairway with square posts and molded edge planks, instead of the more common balusters.

My Road

There's a grassy road awinding
    In my land of long ago,
It leads around the barnyard
    To the river bank below,
On it wanders through the 'Round Field'
    Down a rocky hill I know
Till it seems to gently linger
    Where the salt marsh sedges grow.

Ah, the tang and scent of marshes,
    With the south wind blowing free!
Come the gray tides deep'ning channels
    Creeping inland from the sea;
With my road I pause a moment
    In the view that comes to me
One clear line of western hillsides
    Reaching far as eye can see.

> Grassy road, you oft have called me
>   And I never questioned why!
> I would follow you at morning
>   'Ere the new-mown hay sunned dry;
> When your sunsets, o'er the hilltops
>   Barred with gold your evening sky
> There the length'ning shadows found me
>   We were pals, Road, you and I!
>
>   Agnes Choate Wonson

"At times the hillside was covered with white daisies giving it the appearance of a large white blanket," Agnes described. "Often Sister and I went to the hilltop when we were little girls to help Father at haying time or to sit and listen to stories he shared of earlier island days."

Once when Agnes and her father had walked to the top of the island an unusual incident happened. "Father and I were standing looking toward Maine when suddenly the fog lifted and as clearly as if it were very near, we saw horses and carriages moving about, people sitting in rocking chairs on the porch of the hotel on the Isle of Shoals. It was the only mirage I saw during the years I lived on the island, but it was a remarkable experience, indeed."

Slowly we made our way down the stairs from the attic. We lingered outside on the sloping, grassy knoll as Agnes continued to reminisce. We were filled with gratitude for this preservation of a rich past.

Walking down the slope to the boat, we turned to look once again at the old homestead, staunch and secure, surrounded by ocean, dunes and shimmering marshes. We felt a sense of rightness that this house remains today as a significant example of an unpretentious way of life.

THE ROAD, FERRY & BRIDGE

The Road

Until August 14, 1886 the only access to Choate Island was by boat at high tide, wagon at low and ferry from Dean's Island road. When Lamont Burnham bought one of the farms on the island, he began making plans in 1880 for a bridge. He, Rufus Choate (Agnes' father) and Nehemiah W. Marshall completed these plans and the bridge was ready for use in August 1886. In a diary kept by Rufus Choate, there is a detailed, accurate and often humorous account of its planning, construction, cost, setbacks and upkeep.

Preceding the information about the bridge, there is a description of the construction of a road completed in 1879 and a ferry from Dean's to Choate Island in 1881.

> For many years the owners and occupants of the island farms have joked about a new road by which the island might be reached at high water. Twenty years ago the proposed plans were to fill in the creeks to the Broad marsh and thence by a causeway over the marsh to Hardy Point—or to fill toward's Dean's Island with a bridge over Dean's Channel.
>
> In 1863 a self-appointed committee measured the river from the gravel beach at the Northern end of the Crafts Farm to Lakemans Farm and got the estimate for a bridge. Surveys were easily made but roads would not spring into existence.
>
> The Centennial year 1876 witnesses the commencement of the road enterprise—an enterprise of which the present generation cannot expect to see the completion. The present plan is to prepare a horse wagon road from the Island house through the Round Field and orchard and below the wall along on the marshes to the Southwestern shore of the acre nub. Thence by ferry (when there is tide enough) to Dean's Island and thence over the marsh to Low's Island or Story's small island. This is strictly a private road built wholly in the interest of the south Hog Island farm. It is expected that rackets on the horse

The bridge from Choate Island to Dean's Island was in use until destroyed by strong tidal currents in the Portland Storm in 1898.

and wide-rimmed wheels on the wagon may be necessary for a few years between Low's and Dean's Islands. It is proposed to make a horse path of gravel between these Islands as soon as practicable so that rackets may then be no longer necessary. Eventually it is hoped that gravel enough may be placed outside the horse path to support ordinary wagon wheels. The beginning of the enterprise consists in filling the creek between the island and the acre nub—a distance of 120 feet from the wall to the marsh. For this purpose, Patrick Haggarty (a son of the Emerald Isle) was employed at six dollars a month and his board.

On Saturday, November 25, 1876, the first shovelful of earth was thrown by this son of Erin. A speech was made on the occasion and the wildest enthusiasm prevailed among the bystanders. The dirt flew over the wall merrily until hard pan was struck which cooled down the enthusiasm to a quiet and regular heat.

The gravel which we wheeled into the creek last winter settled down and spread out considerably, leaving it about half way up to the level of the marsh. On November 13, 1877 we commenced work again with two men from Salem. They worked one month. We spent a weekend now leveling the roads above and below the wall on the island along side of the creek and the rest of the month we spent in wheeling gravel and marsh mud onto the causeway across the creek. We also made a horse path of gravel across the nub of the marsh.

The campaign of 1878 is upon the causeway over the marsh between Low's and Dean's Islands. The first idea was to make only a horse path two feet wide and to use wide-rimmed wheels for the wagons. The Spring campaign was devoted to this end. About April 1, we commenced at the Dean's Island end. On this island lot and also on the Western part of the Sam Dodge lot we built the path to keep the gravel in its place. The rest of the distance we cut into the marsh about four inches and laid the boards and gravel below the surface beyond the reach of wind and ice.

The distance from Low's Island to Dean's Island is about 2,575 feet. We purchased refuse hemlock boards of J.T. Langmaid of Salem and of Calvin Putnam of Beverly to the amount of 5,689 feet at a cost (with freight) of $53.23. During a stormy night and by a most unexpectedly high tide we lost probably 500 feet of boards which floated although they were all more or less ballasted with rocks.

For three or four hundred feet from Dean's Island and also from Low's Island the gravel was wheeled onto the boards. On the rest of the road the gravel was wheeled from the ferry boat—it having been brought from the gravel pit on Hog Island and landed in the several creeks. During the spring campaign the boards were laid two feet wide and were covered with gravel during the whole distance excepting perhaps 200 feet at or near the bridge. The stringers for the bridges were cut in Dean's Island and put in their place and secured by posts, much to the comfort of foot passengers during the summer.

The gossips of the town were in full blast during the campaign. Self-appointed committees visited the road by day and by night and returned and reported to their fellow-gossips. Wise men shook their heads and said it would accommodate haymakers as they walked to their marsh lots. The project was discussed on barrels and boxes in grocery stores with more force than elegance and every load of boards which was drawn from the cars to the new road added new fuel to the flames.

We began to widen the road in the Fall campaign, October 17. We proposed to widen out two feet by boards and gravel as in the spring campaign. John Kelleher and Mr. Carr were principally employed. An unusual number of severe South Easters delayed our progress as did also many high tides which remained upon the marsh a number of hours in the day. We finished work November 21 and then had a road four feet wide the entire length. On Tuesday, November 26 rode the white horse back to Dean's Island and back safely over the new road. Boards used in the campaign totaled 5,108 feet at a cost with freight of $31.66. Gossips more quiet during this campaign.

We agreed with Mr. Carr to widen the road from Low's Island to Dean's Island by the job in the Spring campaign. For doing this work of widening it two feet the entire length he was paid $35.00.

The gossips and the standing committee now begin to laugh out of the other side of their mouth and to admit that the road is a success. Mr. Carr completed the work of widening the road two feet about May 31. The road is now six feet wide from Low's to Dean's Island. On Monday, June 2, William Marshall rode over the road to Dean's Island and returned in his buggy wagon. February 9 we carried Mr. William Mears to Dean's Island in the wagon and he found the veins of water with his rod and showed where to dig a well. Estimated that water will be found at a depth of 12 feet. The veins of water do not run exactly across the island but inclining from East and West a trifle. The horse was driven into the stable on Dean's Island for the first time in the wagon, September 9.

About October 1, John Carr and Pat Callahan widened the road near Dean's Island about two feet on each side for a distance in length of about 300 feet. This makes the road 10 feet wide. They also graveled a piece on the black grass at the Eastern end of Dean's Island as the road goes to the river. For this work, paid Mr. Carr (about 6 ½ days) $8.00, Mr. Callahan (3 days) $3.75. Henry Burnham was employed to drain off the fresh water from the three acre lot of marsh on Hog Island over which the road is to run. This required 28 rods of ditching at .08, a total cost of $2.24.

The total cost of the road was $566.86. A detailed, dated account of expenses was listed in Rufus Choate's diary. Excerpts from this list include:

December, 1876	Two dirt wheelbarrows @ 2.50 each	$5.00
	One pick axe	.75
	Powder and fuse for blasting bank	.45
	Sharpening drill	.05
	Pay Patrick one month's wages	6.00
January, 1877	One shovel	1.20
	Steeling and sharpening pick axe	.40
May, 1877	Ditching for road & filling holes	2.00
Spring, 1879	Oats for horses	.13

The bridge from Choate Island to Dean's Island, built in 1886 by Rufus Choate, Lamont Burnham and Nehemiah Marshall.

The Ferry

On the 22nd of April, 1881 a cable was stretched across the river from Dean's Island to the nub of marsh on the Hog Island shore. The part which laid over the old town road was wire rope. A small dock was prepared at both landings up which a horse and wagon could go. The ferryboat had a drop on both ends. This boat was built for the purpose in 1878 (costing $100.00) being shoal and flat-bottomed and having a deck and also iron posts and railing. This boat was built on the barn floor in the barn in the village in the winter of 1877-1878 by R. Choate and Mr. Allen Andrews.

On Saturday, 23rd of April, 1881 the ferry boat was run across the river on its regular route three times amid *cheers, speeches and immense enthusiasm*! On Tuesday, May 31, we crossed the ferry three times with the horse with *speeches, waving of hats and nine cheers by the bystanders*. On Sunday, June 19, 1881 Rufus Choate and wife went to a meeting over the ferry, Mrs. Choate not getting out of the carriage from the time of leaving the island house until reaching the house in the village. They returned the same way at night. On the 22nd, we attended a strawberry festival in the evening by the use of the ferry.

Excerpts from the listed expense of building the ferry are:

January, 1880	One day's wages for hauling gravel from pit in orchard on island	$1.00
	Horse and drag for hauling	.50
June 23, 1882	J. Kelleher labor	1.25
	Horse	1.00
January 2, 1883	Hauling gravel onto the dump; horse	.50

THE ROAD, FERRY & BRIDGE

The Bridge

On Friday, January 30, 1880 Lamont G. Burnham, Rufus Choate and Nehemiah C. Marshall petitioned the Legislature for leave to bridge the river at Dean's Island. On Friday, 13 of February the petitioners were granted a hearing and the town of Essex was notified. L.G. Burnham and R. Choate appeared before the committee. No opposition was shown and the legislature gave us a grant, subject to the approval of the Harbor Commissioners. The Harbor Commissioners having notified the town, gave us a hearing, L. G. Burnham and R. Choate appearing before them and gave the petitioners the right to build the bridge without a draw.

Previous to the town meeting in March, 1885, an article was inserted in the warrant to see if the town would allow the owners of the Hog Island farms to build a new road across the present town way. At the meeting (Capt. Charles Howes, moderator), after a statement by R. Choate, the town left the matter in the hands of the selectmen and Mr. Josiah Low. This was virtually giving the consent of the town.

Although the charter was granted in 1880, some causes operated to hinder the pushing of the enterprise until 1884. The winter of 1884 and '85 was spent by Marshall and Choate in gravelling the road alongside of Hog Island on the marsh and in building the road from Hog Island to the bank of the river. The proposed plan during the month and years previous to 1885 was to build the part over the flats in the river mostly of gravel from Hog Island with rocks down the sides to protect it from the wash of the sea. The channels were to be furnished with spile bridges—Dean's Channel bridge 200 feet long and Hog Island channel bridge 100 feet long. One plan for building over the flats was with spiles and plank which was finally adopted. This plan was proposed from the beginning.

On the 20th of June, 1885, Mr. Marshall and Mr. Choate met Mr. Burnham at Mr. Burnham's house at the North End and then adjourned to Low's Island. At that place Mr. Burnham made the offer to build across the river from Dean's to Hog Island in the manner last specified for $1,000.00 each from Marshall and Choate or he would give either Marshall or Choate $1,000.00 for building his third of the same. One month was given for considering the matter. On July 16, Marshall and Choate made the final decision of the question and informed Mr. Burnham that they accepted his offer to build across the river. The remainder of the road was to be built at the equal expense of the three farms and R. Choate was to be allowed $500.00 for what he had already done on the marsh road before the others commenced.

A contract was drawn up by a Boston lawyer and was sworn to before magistrates by which Choate and Marshall were bound and holden to pay to Burnham $1,000.00 each for the bridge and by which each of the three parties were bound to the other two to do each his part in building the rest of the road on both sides of the river. If either party was in default in his share of teaming and labor, it should be made up in money. The contract required the road and bridge to be completed so as to be passable on November 1, 1886.

It was expected at the time of the contract that spruce plank would be used for the sides of the bulkheads. The contract required the bulkheads to be filled with mud to the level of the adjoining marsh while the bridges were to be built above all tides. It was intended at a later day to raise the mud in the bulkheads to a level with the bridges.

The three parties to the contract conveyed each to the other two a right of way over the land covered by the new road so far as owned by each, subject to no bars or gates. William Marshall in consideration of a right of way over the same conveyed land itself in his possession over which the road passed to Burnham, Marshall and Choate. Deeds of rights of way were also obtained of Mrs. Asenath Johnson, the heirs of Job Burnham and the heirs of Nehemiah Dodge.

The new road so far as Choate was responsible reached from Northern Avenue at the North End to the old road which runs up river to the house of Rufus Choate on Hog Island. Marshall and Burnham in addition to these limits were to maintain the road to their farms, a right of way being given them by Rufus Choate.

On Thursday, September 17, 1885, the schooner *Blythe* (Capt. Messinger from Belliveaus Cove, Nova Scotia) arrived at the mouth of Essex River with 426 spruce spiles and the next day anchored below Cross's Island. The vessel was grounded on Conomo Point and the spiles hauled out of her by teams and were rafted to Hog Island and moored in the cove between the farms of Marshall and Choate for the winter. The Island folks prepared to fire a salute on the arrival at the Island of the first raft of spiles, but the raft grounded on a sand spit near Dilly Island just before sundown and did not arrive at the cove until nearly midnight, too late for a demonstration. On the night of Tuesday, September 29, two rafts of spiles broke away from their moorings in the cove and went down the river. They were seen by clammers at daybreak at the mouth of the river. There the rafts broke up and the spiles were thrown upon the beaches, mostly on Castle Neck. Many teams of many men were employed in hauling them to the water and rafting them back again.

On Saturday, December 12, 1885, a cargo of hard pine was expected to arrive from Boston but she spent Saturday night in Rockport harbor. Sunday she arrived (the lighter *Eureka*) in tow of a tug with a cargo of hard pine plank, stringers, caps, etc. and landed at Dean's Island at the south end of the proposed bridge. On Monday about 25 men (mostly from shipyards) were employed unloading the vessel and piling the lumber up by the woods on Dean's Island above the tides. Fifteen men finished unloading about noon the second day and the Lighter went out in the tide. On Tuesday, May 18, 1886, the schooner *Blythe* arrived again in the mouth of Essex River and unloaded the remainder of the spiles and they were rafted to the bridge soon after. On Sunday evening, June 27, the last cargo of lumber for the bridge

A trip to Choate Island by car on frozen Essex River.

arrived at Dean's Island and was unloaded next day. Some more lumber was brought to town on the cars at a later day and teamed to the bridge or floated in rafts.

Mr. Burnham employed Mr. Isaac Deering of Gloucester to build the bridge. The following are the names of the men employed on the work: Isaac Deering, Francis Patterson, Capt. Eben Davis, Henry Montgomery, Joseph Babine, John Malanson and Hardy Burnham. They boarded on the island with Rufus Choate. On Saturday, May 1, 1886, the spile driver *Hope* was towed from Gloucester through the cut by a steam water boat and anchored in Castle Neck Channel abreast of 'Wheeler'. In the evening on the next flood tide, the men towed her to the place of operation.

Henry Montgomery was engineer and fireman and Joseph Babine took his place at the top of the spile driver while driving spiles. Water for the boiler was obtained at first from Mr. Marshall's well near the cottage and later from the springs under the great oak tree near the eastern end of the bridge.

The building of the bridge occupied the time from May 1, 1886, until August 14. On Saturday afternoon, August 14, Mr. Burnham was present with his carriage and when the last plank was laid drove across to Hog Island and returned. He was the first passenger over the bridge. Rufus Choate being in town that p.m. returned over the bridge at night. The next day, August 15, all went to a meeting and returned over the bridge. On Wednesday night, August 18, the spile driver left the river and went again through the cut to Gloucester. The railing to the bridge was put up by Joseph

Procter, Jr. Mr. Walter Parker had charge of the work of filling the bulkheads with mud. About 15 men and 7 horses and carts were employed in this work. The mud was taken from the thatch banks on the Hog Island side and from 'horse bank' between the channels and from Dean's Island and from 'great bank' in canoes.

Obstacles and Discouragements

The bridge was commenced at the Eastern end. For many years previously the channel between Hog Island and the 'Great Bank' had been filling up and the bed of the river was completely bare at low water. A large basin of water near the spot where the bridge was commenced was obliged to empty itself at low water into the 'wading place' channel and thence into Dean's Channel. The filling the Eastern bulkhead with mud interfered with this natural outlet and the water now forced its way alongside the spiles and plank and also between the two rows of spiles and plank before the space could be filled, gouging out the mud and sand at the bottom of the river to the depth of 6 to 8 feet thus doubling the amount of mud necessary to fill the space for the roadway. This rushing of the tide for two hours just before low water, washing out the sand from around the spiles, undermined some of them so that their power of resisting the sea was weakened.

Before beginning the bridge, the 'wading place' channel where the bridge was to stand was so shoal that at the lowest tide a man could walk across it without going over the tops of rubber boots. On filling the bulkheads on both sides of this bridge the water was forced through the bridge with such power that the channel was at once scooped out to the depth of 6 or 8 feet and thousands of tons of sand were deposited in a large bank just above the bridge. Some of the bridge spiles were started from their bed and a few were replaced by oak spiles. One hundred tons more of rocks were brought to this bridge and were used to pave the bottom of the channel around the spiles to prevent further washing. Two breakwaters—three cornered, built of spiles and plank and filled with mud were built at each end of the short bridge on the lower side to stiffen the whole structure. So great was the rush of water under this bridge that it was decided to make the long bridge nearly 500 feet long.

Necessity is the mother of invention. The bulkhead across 'horse bank' was filled with mud from the thatch bank North West of the road. Timbers were sloped up onto the road bed and planked over and the teams hauled up the mud at low water. Day and night tides were used for this purpose. Lanterns were called for by night. Horses were stabled on the roadway at high water. A canvas was stretched over them, held up by the spiles. On this canvas the men slept and another sailcloth was stretched above them to keep them dry. Hay, grain and water were brought across from Dean's Island to the horses in boats, the Dean's River bridge not being finished at that time. The eastern end of the bulkhead across 'horse bank' was also badly washed by the tide before it could be filled, thus vastly increasing the amount of mud to fill it. On approaching the channel in Dean's River while driving the bridge spiles, a ledge was encountered which reached entirely to Dean's Island and gradually approached the surface as it advanced towards the island. East of the channel, the spiles were considered to be driven firmly enough but West of the channel it was found necessary to stiffen them by building a 'crib' and filling it with rocks.

Mr. Burnham with indomitable perseverance and abundant means at command, overcame all difficulties and discouragements and triumphed in the face of all obstacles.

SUPERSTITUIONS, TALES & WITCHCRAFT

After a trip to the island in 1899, a visitor wrote in the guest book:

> And now I know how fair the winds
> Across Choate Island blow
> And how, about the storied house
> The great tales come and go.

Especially on rainy days when everyone was forced to stay inside, groups sat enthralled as they listened to tales and stories of the early island days. The island was closely connected with the witchcraft tragedy in the Salem jail and on Gallows Hill. Thomas Choate's wife, Mary Varney, was a niece of John Proctor who was executed on August 19, 1692. Thomas was one of thirty brave men who signed a petition in his behalf and witnessed his will while he was in prison, his wrists in manacles. It was a time when "anyone who expressed sympathy with accused persons or doubted their guilt was exposed to danger. Men spoke in whispers. Each one feared to meet another's eye."

This fear, apprehension and even belief in witches was revealed in the witchcraft stories on the island for many years after the executions ceased. Some early settlers believed that witches would take the family horse out of the barn on dark nights and ride him until reeking with sweat leaving him early the next morning tied to a post "all a lather." Other Chebacco area stories included one of Captain Osborn who was returning to Manchester one night, looked up and saw a horse with two women on its back going over the tree tops. He knew the women, fainted dead away and remained insensible for a long time.

As a little girl Agnes remembered the tales of superstition handed down from other generations through family records. Some of these are stories of strange and unexplainable happenings on the island. One concerned a fisherman who sailed from the island but never returned. It was believed the house was haunted by his ghost who, in the dark of night, could be heard coming up the stairs with his boots full of water.

It was believed that there were foreboding signs which hung over every household like a gloomy cloud. The story has been told about Mrs. Mary Giddings Choate (wife of William on the island) that once she went in the cellar to draw cider from a barrel. As she was about to draw, three distinct raps were heard on the other end of the barrel. She immediately rapped three times when to her astonishment three more raps followed. She confessed it made her "hair stand on end." This was believed to be an omen and "there was death in the house soon after."

In 1784 while in his chamber dressing for his wedding to Mary Cogswell, David Choate, Sr. heard a strange sound which resembled "dirt falling into a coffin. In less than two months his wife was in her grave." A short time before David moved from the island to the village, carpenters were at work shingling the eastern end of the island house. Very early one morning three raps were heard. At breakfast the workmen and family were talking the matter over and someone suggested that it was one of the carpenters knocking. Sarah Choate, sister of David, replied with great solemnity, "It was my death call." She died a year later.

Mrs. Hannah Choate Marshall one day heard a strange noise in the cupboard and on looking there found a tumbler cracked from top to bottom on opposite sides, the two halves still standing in place. It was considered a bad omen and her son, Nehemiah, was soon after found dead in the shop on the southerly end of the island.

One of Agnes' favorite stories was told by her father about Eph Frank Mears' gift with the "Divining Rod."

"In my day," her father began, "when anyone wanted to dig a well, Eph Frank was called upon. He would cut himself a forked stick, of hazelwood if possible, but any forked twig would do."

Eph Frank would be told the approximate place where they would like the well to be. Then grasping the handles of the fork, holding it erect, he walked slowly back and forth and all around the desired spot, looking for the vein of water many feet deep underground. It was believed that because he had that gift, the forked stick would slowly, but powerfully turn over in his hands whenever he crossed any such vein. He would offer to let anyone try to hold back the stick to keep it from twisting. By crossing and recrossing, the exact spot could be determined where the vein of water was flowing. However, much to the disappointment and expense of those digging wells, the only drawback in his talent was his inadequacy in telling how deep down the vein flowed or how much rocky ledge there was to interfere with digging.

Agnes' father was a firm believer in lightning rods and had one installed on the long barn directly on the roof over the spot where he thought a vein of water flowed. Once he had Eph verify this vein by walking back and forth, his stick turning quickly in his hands. Further proof of the rod's correct placement was evidenced by

Eph on one of his island visits when lightning struck the barn, went down the rod behind the cows by a full haymow into the ground toward the vein of water.

As a little girl, Agnes felt a sense of adventure when her father told her about buried treasures on the island. "Long ago it was believed that Captain Kidd's pirates buried gold under the old juniper tree on the southern side of the pasture hill. Now if only a forked stick could tell us the truth about that!" he chuckled.

In later years, many visitors to the island tried dousing for the gold using crudely constructed metal detectors. The treasure, if any, remains buried to this day.

Stories of drowning were told usually during the storms with the wind sweeping across the island, rain beating against the house, the ocean pounding on the shore. One incident which occurred in August, 1792 was described in a family diary:

> "Mr. Benjamin Procter living on the lower farm fell from his horse soon after entering the creek at the mouth of the first small creek on the left as you go to the island and was found a few minutes after with his face in a small puddle of water dead. He was nearly 80 years of age and probably fell in a fit."

Another drowning in 1872 in which two members of the Choate family joined in the search was described in the family diary and reported in the *Salem Gazette*:

> "The sad accident now recorded occurred on Friday morning, November 29, 1872, between six and eight o'clock when Mrs. Emma Barker Celby was drowned on the Broad Marshes. Mrs. Celby was in April last married to Sidney Celby, son of the tenant on the south farm on Hog Island. She was but 18 years of age but was taller and larger than most females of adult years. After their marriage, they spent most of the summers and falls on the farm.
>
> On Friday morning the wind was South East which brought the tide in earlier than usual, the weather cloudy but not cold. It was low water about four o'clock. At six when the tide was over the road, Mr. Richard Celby with his daughter-in-law started in the wagon for Ipswich. They had several bags of grain for the mill which made a heavy load. Although the tide was high they safely crossed the 'wading place' and kept the road, until they came to the bold bank opposite Dean's Island between which the spot is notorious for mud and mire. Here they lost the road being about ten feet too near the bank. As the wheels went down, the horse struggled and sprang forward breaking both traces.
>
> The tide was rising rapidly and was then knee deep in the road. Mr. Celby carried his daughter to the marsh and told her to stay there until he came for her with a boat. She was placed upon the marsh dry and comfortable and was so far above the tide that it could not have reached her for three hours and could

only have covered her ankles at high water. Had she obeyed the instructions to remain, this sad record would not have been made. She was full of fears when Mr. Celby left with the horse but promised to come for her with a boat. At that time it was growing light although half an hour before sunrise.

Mr. Celby mounted the horse and rode to the mainland there leaving his horse with Mr. Hardy commenced the laborious work of dragging the boat from the canal near his house to the creek near Low's Island. This probably took about an hour and a half before he returned again to the wagon. Once arriving at the marsh Mrs. Celby was nowhere to be found nor seen over the entire Broad Marsh. Mr. Celby at once examined the small creek adjoining and passed over acres of the Broad Marsh calling her name. After a fruitless search, he went to the island and sent his youngest son to renew the search. On the causeway leading from the island to the mainland he found what he believed to be her footsteps pointing in the direction of Ipswich. This quieted his fears since this was beyond the reach of the tide.

At noon on Friday rain commenced falling with the wind Southeast and blowing heavily. On Saturday the wind blew a gale from the Westward and was extremely cold. On Sunday the weather had moderated. On Monday nothing had been heard from Mrs. Celby. No one of all her friends in Ipswich had seen her nor her brother in Hamilton. A bitter Northwest wind was blowing but search on the Broad Marsh was now resumed by Mr. Celby, Mr. Burnham and William Choate. R. Choate hastened to the town and informed the Selectmen of the probable loss and the bell was rung and news spread rapidly. The tide was too high so the search was abandoned until the next morning. Mr. Celby was walking home towards Hog Island on the Broad Marsh opposite Round Island when he discovered the dead body lying in the marsh near the salt pond.

On Thursday, Dec. 5 the coroner held an inquest in the small room in the basement of the North Church and the jury rendered a verdict of accidental drowning. Probably the young woman found the minutes of waiting seemed like hours and becoming panic-stricken attempted to find her way off through the water though she had been left in a dry place."

There were many Indian tales told during island days. Agnes remembers one story especially:

"Every year when Father hayed the Hill Field, we'd talk of Indian days. It is difficult to imagine our island in those old Indian days: wigwams over it, with the Fort on top. Looking towards Maine, we could imagine how the Indians saw the first war canoes of the Tarrantines coming in the mouth of the river. Our Indian tribe was the Agawams and always friendly to the white people. They lived by fishing and clamming. Father once had me dig almost a foot down just below the bank and I found nothing but clam shells.

Heart-break Hill is over Ipswich way. The story is told of an Indian girl who fell in love with an Englishman. He promised to return to her but never did. She died of a broken heart, thus the name of the hill."

Another story told to the guests was that of the firing of a cannon ball on one of the island barns in 1812.

"For many years we had proof-for-the-showing of the effect of the war with England of 1812. The island was divided into three farms; ours, the largest with pasture, the middle called the Marshall Farm and the lower called the Burnham Farm. One of the large barns on the Marshall Farm had a hole made by a cannon ball which was never repaired and a source of 'show and tell' interest to visitors. For some reason, a British Frigate got into Ipswich harbor and to let us know what war is all about, fired a cannon ball on the island, striking the barn in the peak of one end, leaving a huge hole. A popular walk on Sunday afternoons was one to exhibit the gaping evidence. Other than this one incident, our island was never affected by war."

Choate house side entrance. Sand dunes in the background.

About the time of the Revolutionary War when the island was covered with dense woods at one end, a mare was pastured there by someone from the mainland. In the fall when the animal was removed, there was no suspicion that the mare had become a mother of a young colt. The next spring, the colt was found on the island alive and well. Using the thicket as shelter and stable, he was well protected. By pawing the snow, he had reached grass and survived the long winter.

"No matter how often we repeated these stories," Agnes assured us, "each telling seemed an exciting adventure to all who visited the island. We never tired of show and tell."

NEW-MOWN HAY

Early inhabitants of Choate Island turned it into an agricultural farmland raising sheep and crops of corn, potatoes, onions and other vegetables. For many years, islanders dried fish on the beaches which were many feet deep with clam shells left by the Indians. During the summers Agnes lived on the island, her father sold vegetables, hay, butter, milk and eggs. To transport the produce, he built and operated a ferry pulling himself with ropes and pullies.

In an 1875 diary he kept detailed records of planting, harvesting and selling a crop of onions in the "field before the house," a choice spot 145' long and 76' wide in full sun, the surrounding trees providing protection from the Northwest winds. He recorded that after spreading five full ox carts of green manure on April 27, harrowing the bed and spreading two loads of year-old and rotted manure the next day, he raked and wheeled off stones and planted sixty-four rows! After many battles with the dodder weed which wound and choked the roots and onion tops, midgets "swarming in battalions", heaviest rain in years in May which washed out several rows and deposited gravel from the new road on one third of the onion bed, drought in August, the crop was raked into rows on September 8 and turned each day until dry. The harvest yield was 110 bushels, mostly for use on the island and at the mainland home; some sold at $1.00 a bushel!

At one time the island was divided into three farms. Benjamin Proctor, a relative of Mrs. Thomas Choate, purchased the more northerly part of the island from Henry Bennett. This farm remained in the Proctor family for nearly 100 years. About 1795 it was purchased by the Choates then resold in 1802 to Mr Jonathan Story, remaining in the Story family until about 1879 when purchased by Lamont G. Burnham Esq. of Boston. This section of the island was known as the Burnham Farm.

The middle island farm was purchased from the Choates in 1805 by William Cogswell then resold in 1810 to Moses Marshall, whose wife was Hannah Choate. This section, known as the Marshall Farm, lay between Burnham Farm and the original Choate Farm.

For over 200 years, members of the Choate family farmed the island land. During the years Agnes lived on the island, a big event was haying which filled the atmosphere with the sweet aroma of new-mown hay, transforming the tawny fields into a place of haunting, spicy fragrance.

Mowing Time

Across the tawny summer fields
    Drift scents of long ago.
The warm, sweet breath of new-mown hay
Calls from the years of yesterday
    A farm I used to know.

I vision those unhurried dawns
    Calm rising from the sea.
The wind-swept field reached to the shore
Where ruffled waves in morns of yore
    Shook shaggy manes at me.

My father mowed those browsy slopes
    Before the sun was high.
The dried sweet odors of the air
With spicy fragrance everywhere
    Will haunt me till I die.

I wonder if those sleeping fields
    Were cut this year and dried,
And if the sunshine-scented hay
In long sleep, dreams the days away,
    An old gray barn inside.

    Agnes Choate Wonson

Agnes remembers that when a little girl, to earn extra money for Christmas she and her sister, Celia, would pick the prolific white daisy (which her father considered a white weed) on the day before haymowing. They earned one cent a hundred! The day after daisy picking, the hay was cut and tossed on top of the hay rack and Agnes and Celia were lifted high in the air to the top of the pile to tread it down, earning two cents a load.

"Father always left the 'Hill Field' for the last cutting," Agnes reminisced. "It was long and rambling, exactly on top of our island farm with rocky pasture land all around it, and between it and the lower hay fields. The crop was generally light, so our part of the work was easy. Father let Dolly Brown (every horse we had, he called the same name) stand and wait while Sister and I picked white everlasting and goldenrod to take to mother. Often we sat on top of one of the haycocks and listened to father's stories of the island.

"Reluctantly the last 'scatterings' of hay were gathered. We were hoisted on top and Dolly Brown started down the hill to the barn, the sun lower now and the sea gulls flocking towards the dunes for the night. The days were growing shorter already, and how the crickets sounded like Fall! Each year we looked forward to the island top in the hayrack, especially if it was a cool, easterly cloudy day and we could snuggle down in the fragrant loads in the ride down the hill to the barn. Even now it seems I can feel the warmth of the sun, smell the elusive scents. I tried to capture it all in a poem."

New-Mown Hay

If I could only catch
    Between my hands
Elusive scents, rich full-blown scents
    Of new-mown hay…
I'd hold that fragrance
    Of the meadow lands,
That though the flying summers fade
    'Twould with me stay!

If I could only make this poem fling
    Those sun-touched scents of
Shadeless fields
    To you, who read…
What moving memories
    Of olden days 'twould bring
Of childhood's happy summers
    So dear indeed!

Agnes Choate Wonson

The hay was stored in the island barn, a one-story structure 90' long, 25' wide with hay mows on either side. According to a diary kept by Agnes' father, Rufus Choate,

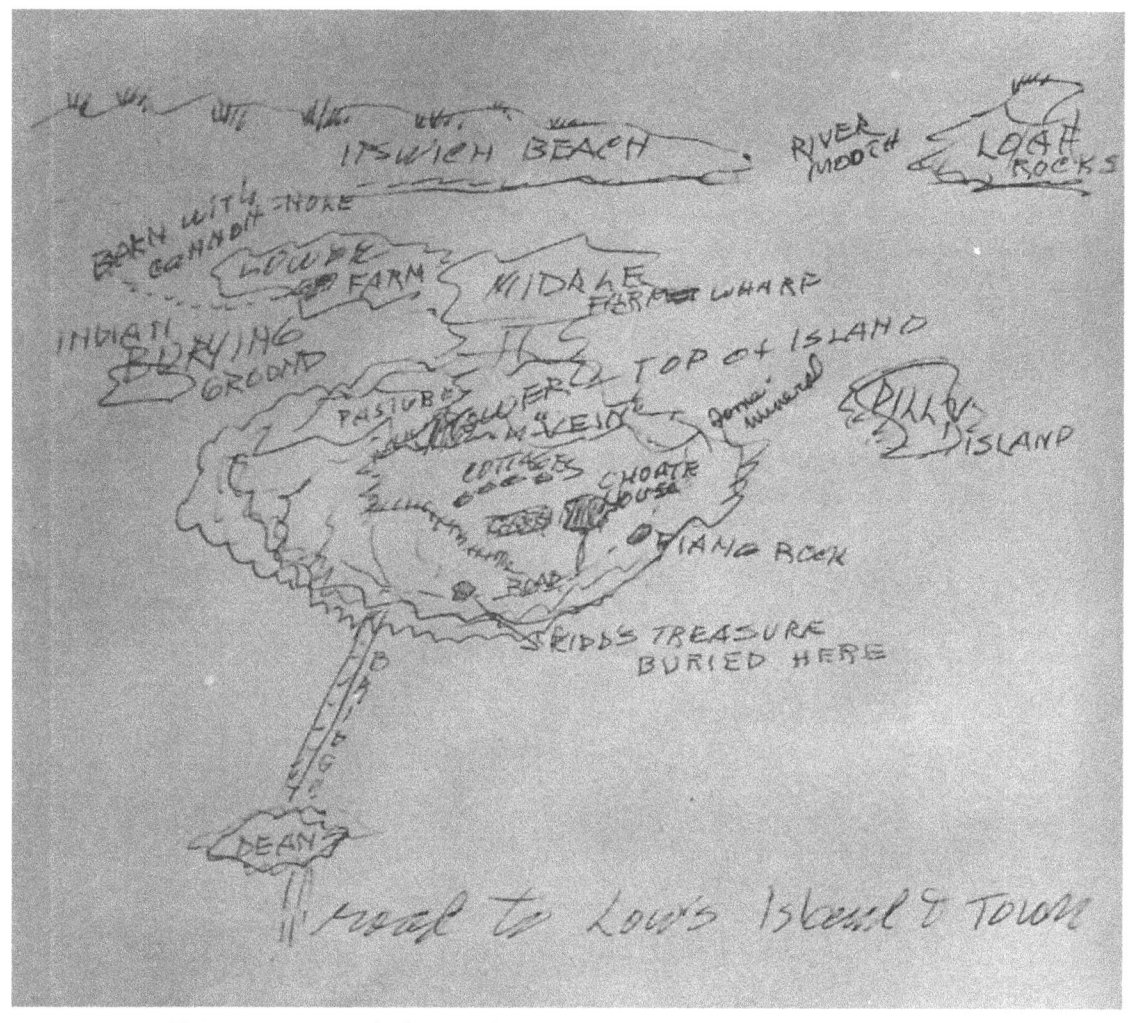

"Memory map" of Choate Island drawn by Agnes Choate Wonson in her 98th year.

the barn "…was built almost entirely of oak, nearly every timber was oak. The corner and the other posts were eight inches square; the rafters and plate of oak."

There was a cow yard before the barn reaching a little to westward of the barn towards the round field. A cider mill was west of the yard. Rufus recorded that "in the great gale of 1815, the upper corner post next to the house and an upper post next to it broke and the barn moved up hill."

> "I remember our old hay barn on the island," recalls Agnes. "It was shingled, gray and weathered. How my sister and I used to love to race back and forth its whole length between the dusty, sweet-smelling hay mows. Under them were the horse stalls and cow stanchions and a hen pen at one end. The barn was built in 1775. Under the barn roof among the worm-holed rafters, swallows

built their nests. Father said the same flocks of birds came back year after year. Sister and I loved to lie on the haymows and listen to their chattering and watch their skimming flight in and out the wide doors at each end of the barn.

My Father always kept two Jersey cows; he said he liked their thick cream on his oatmeal each morning. With the hens he always kept four ducks. I remember often they would each lay an egg just in time for breakfast. We thought Father specially trained them! Sister and I each had pet hens one year, grown from tiny chicks. I remember mine was called Yellow Breast and was so tame she would come to me when I called and would jump into my lap and cuddle down like a kitten."

The barn became a main point of interest for Agnes and her sister when taking guests on exploratory tours. Stories their father told were passed on to visitors. One tale was a sad account of twin daughters of the slave, Ned. After a corn husking party, the girls decided to sleep the night in the barn, became ill with pneumonia and died. Their graves are on the island. Visitors were shown splintered rafters and posts in the barn, evidence that the building had been struck by lightning on Sunday evening, June 25, 1875. In a family diary is the following description which Agnes and her sister retold to their guests:

One evening a shower passed the northern part of Hog Island about 7:30 pm. A bolt struck the peak of the upper barn at the western end, divided and passed down both rafters and both corner posts. On the North side it nearly shattered the rafter, tore off the weather board, split off the corner boards which cover the corner post and split off the outer corner of the post from the eaves to the ground. The front rafter was somewhat shattered and the post to the ground was scored. Amazing there was no fire.

Even in the winter the old barn cast a spell.

The Barn in Winter

> Nestled midst a waste of snow
>   With wide door facing toward the sea
> Whose gray-robed waves sweep to and fro
>   The old barn calmly waits for me.
>
> Patient through many years, has kept
>   Its trysting by the river shore
> 'Neath lonely winter clouds, it slept
>   Till waked by dew-starred blooms once more.

A little child, long years ago,
    'Mid fragrant mows once loved to lie
And watch the skimming swallows go.
    Old barn, that little child was I!

I'll let the world go by, some day
    And o'er the grass-grown road to you
Past woodbined wall, I'll find the way
    And bring the time of dreams come true.

              Agnes Choate Wonson

A SUMMER PLAYGROUND

When Agnes' father stated the magical words "time to move on," days of excited preparation to go to the island began. Agnes remembers:

> "Come Spring, we packed all our summer belongings including the churn, trunks, boxes, crates, necessary staples and even Mother's sewing machine, for it was during the summer she made our clothes for school. Everything was loaded on the hay rack, our cows tied behind and off we went to our island.
>
> Each year Mr. Watson staked out a road over the riverbed to use at low tide, but we had to ford 'deep hole wading place' channel. If we got a late start and the tide started coming in, the wagon would float and the horses pulling the hay rack and the cows trailing behind had to swim. Of course, my sister and I thought this great fun and were delighted!"

Many island visitors took this Cherry Lane road also. Miriam Choate, a cousin of Agnes, described the trip as seeming "a route of peril if meeting another team or load of hay. Drivers had to back the horses to a turn out—a problem of almost tragic possibilities if not an expert driver or unused to horses."

When Agnes and her sister Celia were children, the happy summer days were spent vaulting fences, making potato people, digging clay on nearby Corn Island for molding animals and flowers, treading hay, swimming, digging on the shore trying to find the start of the layers of clam shells left by the Indians, hours filled with music. But a special treat for Agnes each summer was the trip to Dilly Island to get salt hay. She described it:

> "I always remember how Father fed his cows—English hay while it lasted then finished with salt hay. Milk always had a bit of a salty taste during the season. Dilly Island was our spot for cutting salt hay. If Father had no hired man to help him, I always chose to go along in his place. (I wonder if Father ever regretted I wasn't a boy?)

Agnes and three friends vaulting the fence on Choate Island.

When the right tide came, Father would row over to Dilly and cut all he could with a scythe, then rake it up out of tidal reach, leaving it for a few days to dry. Then came the part I liked. Mother packed a lunch of dried beef sandwiches, sugared gingerbread squares and Father's favorite drink of molasses-sweetened water in a two quart container. Off we went for Dilly, the long hay poles sticking out over the stern of the rowboat each side of me in the stern seat.

'Trim the boat, Little Girl,' Father began as he started to row. 'Keep the Dilly trees in line off the bow.' Soon we reached Dilly Island, a small somewhat wooded rise of land connected by marsh to Corn Island opposite our island home. Landing and pulling up the boat out of tidal reach was first; then, while Father raked up the dried salt grass and cocked it, I did what I loved to do— gathered 'sweet grass.' Below the trees in the island center was a long green shining stretch of fragrant smelling grass. I soon had great sweet-smelling bunches tied together by some of its own fragrant blades to hang from our mantels on the island. How I still remember that fragrance!

Meanwhile, the hay having been cocked, Father would run the two poles nearly together, placing himself between those on one end with me doing the same on the other side of the cock. Carefully lifting both poles, the hay cock was carried and dumped in the rowboat. This took not more than an hour with frequent rests and queries from Father. 'Tired, Little Girl?' Since only two or three cocks could be carried to the island at a time, imagine the number of exciting trips we made for several days. On arrival at our island the hay load had to be pitched out and recocked for the trip up to the barn.

At lunchtime we settled ourselves comfortably amidst the salty-marshy odors while gray gulls circled over the last clam flats left by the flooding tide. Late clammers were being borne rapidly upstream by swift in-coming current.

> 'Now the tide will soon be flood and Mother will be looking for us, Little Girl. Pick up the can and lunch basket and we'll row back to the island. See, there's Mother now, waving to us from the piazza.'"

The weather on the island in summer varied from year to year. Agnes' father noted in an 1873 diary that Mr. R. Channel remembered a summer he rented land for a corn crop. His four acres of corn back of the barn was worthless because it was so cold that milk froze in August.

The Essex Echo reported in August, 1889 that "after the storm on Choate Island, Mr. Rufus Choate went out and secured hailstones sufficient to freeze a lot of ice cream."

Somehow, whatever the weather, nothing spoiled the fun of living on the island for Agnes and her sister. On bright sunny days they swam and raced over the hills, stopping to pick daisies or to lie in them watching the clouds 'scurry above.' On stormy or cold days they played inside, exploring secret passageways and creating their own pastimes. A favorite game was playing 'house' at Piano Rock on the island. It was located below the homestead on the rocky bank of the river under shade of the old bass woods. Agnes remembers:

> "The piano had a very real-looking keyboard, with two little rocks below for the pedals. This was in the 'parlor.' A big flat rock with a high back made a comfortable arm chair. A low flat rock was the table. Here we always kept our treasures. I remember there was a pink starfish, a gray lucky stone with a white line all around it and best of all, a round fishing net cork that had a hole in the

Bungalow, one of the guest cottages when Agnes summered on the Island.

A SUMMER PLAYGROUND

Summer guests arriving on the island for a party.

middle. A stubby stick fitted inside like a candle. The fireplace was beneath a rock that hung over like a shelf. Below, sticks were piled like real logs, and a curving line of clam shells marked the edge of the hearth.

Just below, a huge rock was the kitchen. The flat top was the table and a little nook on one side was the cupboard. Pieces of shells and shiny pebbles were dishes. A soft dried thistle-top made a dish mop and some ragged pieces of a torn sail were the towels. A gnarled apple tree near by was the stable. A low spreading branch was the horse. I remember we used seaweed for reins."

Even during the late 1700's when William Choate and his family lived on the island, there were many parties with summer guests and residents. At one time alone there were sixteen marriageable young ladies on the island, five of them daughters of William. An amusing story is told of a Mr. Baker who "crossed the creek to Hog Island on a courting expedition. With embarrassment, the young man looked about and making a bold push said, 'I've come a-courting. Which girl shall I take?' Mrs. Choate gave him her daughter Mary whom he courted and eventually married. Within a very short time, fifteen other spruce men paddled across the creek from Ipswich, each in turn to find in this isolated place a rosy-cheeked damsel for a wife. Indeed so fashionable was it at that period to go to the island for a wife that when these sixteen pretty girls were all married, one old patriarch who had seen his seventh and last daughter wedded and carried off, with great emotion exclaimed, 'I do believe they'll come for my wife next.' "

It was this same atmosphere of parties, fun and good times with summer guests coming and going when Agnes lived on the island. "It was a thoroughly delightful summer existence," Agnes recalls. "There was a feeling we were all one family sharing happy times."

The well in front of the house was the source of water supply for the Choate families.

Agnes' father built *Tower Cottage* at the foot of the hill facing sand dunes and ocean. The cow path winding in front of the cottage they named Agamenticus Avenue because it pointed to the spot on the horizon where Mt. Agamenticus in Maine rose into view. Four more cottages were built on the west side of the house. "We called them four B's in a row and dubbed them *Bungalow, Binnacle, Barnacle* and *Barber Pole*," Agnes said. The *Bungalow* was built by her Uncle Leavitt Burnham from Omaha and called *Omaha Cottage* until it was sold to Henry Bacon who renamed it *Bungalow*, a fashionable name at the time for a small one-story home. Beside it was the *Binnacle*, built by Frank Ellis Burnham who also built a barn behind the long barn on the island. The cottage, two stories high, was called *Binnacle*—ship talk for "high up." The newer barn was moved up the hill and made into a house christened the *Barnacle*. Henry Bacon sold the *Bungalow* to William Bacon, then built the fourth cottage, *Barber Pole*—so named for its very bright colors.

The cottages were filled at all times with friends: Browns from Worcester, Farnhams of Salem, Fullers of Newton, McKenzies of Waltham, Burnhams from Essex. When someone called out, "Launch rounding the marsh corners!" the words were magic.

"Our visitors would leave Essex on a launch and the flowing tide would bring them to the shore where all of us on the island would rush down the slope to greet them," Agnes explained.

Halfway up the hill from the shore was a bulletin board. It was a point of pride for each to try to out-do the other with cleverly designed signs announcing parties, sings and musicals to be held during the week—outdoors if weather permitted: inside with taffy candy pulls if weather stormy or cold.

Agnes describes a typical day on the island:

> "It all started with a daily swim. At breakfast we decided if it would be diving at high or flood tide, swimming at ebb or half tide or digging for clams at low after a swim. We donned our blousey-bloomered swim suits and ran down the slope. Some of the crowd were fancy divers; personally, I preferred to swim. The one event I can remember was my swimming from our wharf on Choate Island to the mouth of the river (at ebb tide, of course) without touching or stopping once. I was accompanied by a couple of boys in a boat just in case I needed help, but I swam the mile without aid.
>
> After the morning swim, everyone went separate ways to his or her thing. Mine was writing short verses and rhymes and accompanying them with sketches. When I was sixteen some of these were accepted and published by Farm Journal for which I received the great amount of $1.00!
>
> Two other events proved popular. An announcement to go deep-sea fishing the next day always brought a boat full at 5:00 a.m. Deep-sea fishing meant going past the outer buoy and bringing home flat flounder, cod, hake. Once someone dragged in a skate."

On warm evenings there were sings and yearly minstrel shows held on one of the cottage piazzas. Agnes played a banjo (with wire strings instead of cat gut because of the dampness), her sister the mandolin. On Sunday nights everyone crowded into the Choate house parlor for the weekly hymn sing. The accompaniment was an old

The island, a summer playground showing old barn, four summer cottages, plus *Tower Cottage* built by Agnes' father, Rufus. The Choate house was painted white during the years Agnes lived there. Note the long vine-covered porch.

Choate house as it was when Agnes summered on Choate Island.

melodeon which her father purchased at an auction. The instrument had belonged to a popular singing group called the Peakes who performed throughout Europe and the United States. Sunday evening was a happy time, the chorus changing with the arrival of a new group of guests.

The old melodeon played by Agnes' father, Rufus, for hymn sings.

The Old Melodeon

Tide on the ebb, and the gray waves reach
    Their listless arms to the surf-swept sea.
Thick fog, dusk-blown, drifts o'er the beach,
    And the dark night folds in silently.

From the mist-wrapped knoll, does there come a glow
    Shining with fond-remembered cheer?
Do the farmhouse windows warm welcome show
    Just as of old in a long-gone year?

I would that I once again might stand
    On the worn, flat stone before the door;
That my hand might touch your vanished hand
    As I enter the low, square rooms once more.

A sound seems to echo from parlor quaint—
    From the ancient-keyed melodeon there
Come caressing strains of melody faint
    As I pause by the dim-lit narrow stair.

Old tunes, old notes of forgotten song
    In chords are blent, as your magic weaves
Sweet harmonies, Ah, but the years are long;
    For the gentle player my heart still grieves.

Tide on the flood and the light of dawn;
    Calmly the farmhouse waits alone.
Through life's tides bear me on and on
    My heart holds memories all its own.

        Agnes Choate Wonson

On Sundays, church was a must for Agnes and her sister, Celia. Good or bad tide, they packed their best Sunday clothes and with their father rowed to Boyd's landing, changed to their Sunday attire in their home on the mainland and walked to church. It always bothered her father that her mother preferred to stay on the island with the guests!

An amusing story was told by Miriam Choate Hobart, cousin of Agnes, about Mr. Bacon, an island guest who commuted each day from the island to the mainland to catch a train for Boston where he worked.

> "When the tide was high he had no trouble, but during the weeks when the tide ran low early mornings and late afternoons, he was reduced to two means of locomotion—a wheel barrow and a canoe. Where there was enough water he paddled the canoe in which he carried the wheel barrow. When the water grew too shallow for the canoe, he placed it in the wheel barrow and trundled it

Daises covered the lawn in front of *Barber Pole*, a guest cottage.

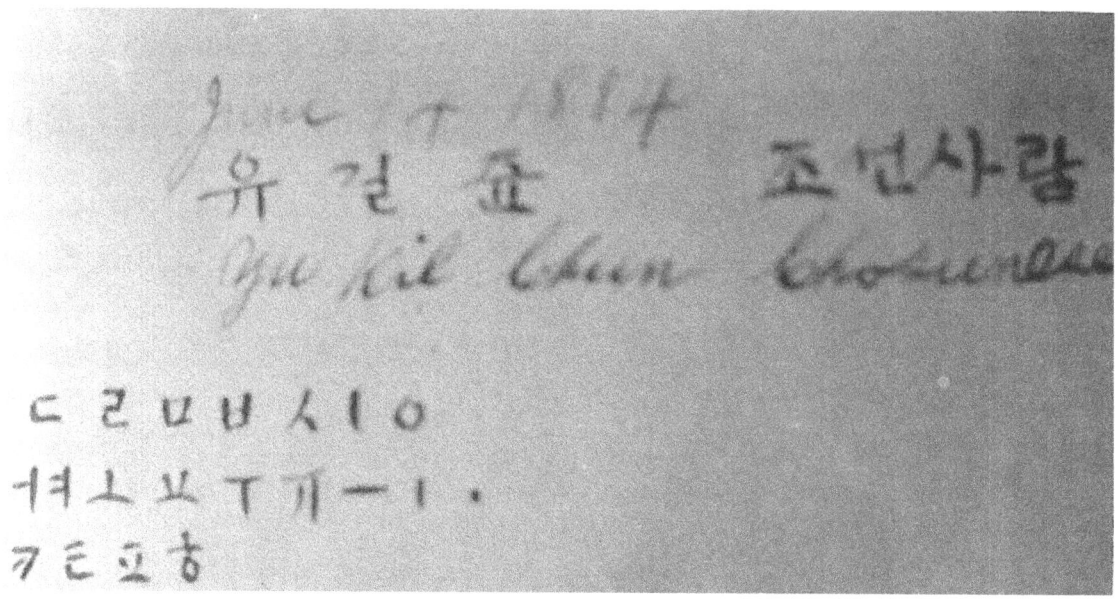

In island guest book is the signature of Yul Kil Chun, attaché for the first Korean Embassy in the United States.

> across the sand bars. By these means he made his way to 'Billy's Point' where he parked canoe and wheel barrow in the bushes until his return trip in the evening."

Originally, guests and visitors to the island climbed the winding stairs to the attic and left their signatures on the large white chimney in the center of the room. "This was designated the 'plastered guest book' until misinterpreted by the prim and proper," Agnes chuckled.

There are many legible inscriptions, including Agnes' when a young girl and that of the author Eugene Field. Beginning on June 16, 1877 a hardback paper book was used on the hall table at the foot of the stairs. As early as 1879 there were visitors registered from Wisconsin, New Jersey, Colorado, New York and Canada. Those signing the book included tourists who came to the birthplace of the famous lawyer, Rufus Choate. There were many poems, quotations and comments. In 1879, Thomas Choate (descendent of the first Choate to settle on the island) noted: "Thomas Choate, of Auburn, New York whose grandfather was born on this island and in this house blest in memory." Yu Kil Chun, an attache of the first Korean embassy in this country signed the guest book on June 14, 1884. Signatures show that groups such as the Mechanics Band and the Clam Chowder Club came to the island to have parties. On August 12, 1898 there was the notation, "Peace with Spain."

In a diary dated 1895, Agnes' mother wrote about parties where guests enjoyed clam

The summer cottages *Bungalow, Binnacle, Barnacle*, and *Barber Pole* remained on the island until removed as part of the restoration plans of Richard Crane, who negotiated for the purchase of the island farm in 1916.

fritters, scalloped clams and ice cream. Before the season ended she recorded the temperature in September as 94° and described trips to Salem in the 'electrics' and to Gloucester by boat. Agnes remembers with amusement how guests reacted to the typical visitor's day menu. Always her mother served clam chowder, crackers and soft custard. Many first-timers thought the chowder only a first course and ate sparingly only to regret it mid-afternoon!

First-timers rarely remained thus. As often as possible they returned to this summer playground to share the fun, laughter, peace and beauty Agnes captured in her poem:

My View

A winding path, up a gentle hill
    Where the fields, new-mown, with fragrance fill,
Past cottage homes, four in a row
    Whose eager eyes o'er seaward go.

Through pasture bars the path climbs on
    Till the top is reached: the "hill-field" won!
At last, my view! Long stretch of sea
    And saffron sand dunes call to me.

To South and West, mauve row on row
    Receding hill slopes fainter grow.
Below, far down, range marshes green
    Where shining shallows wind between.

A bit of a breeze goes smiling by
    And ruffles my hair under the sky.
With one last glance I leave my view
    But it stays in my heart the whole year through!

                Agnes Choate Wonson

EPILOGUE

Island Call

White wind clouds are flying
And seagulls are crying
    Where the river winds down to the sea.
Last fog-veils drift clearer
Past an island grown dearer
    And it calls to the river and me.

        Agnes Choate Wonson

Our tour of Choate Island had ended. Reluctantly we made our way back to the boat; but before pulling anchor, we took one last look at the island's beauty. Our eyes swept the spacious landscape to capture and store in our hearts the memories of this incredible day. The Choate house remained serene and silent as when we landed. Deer poised motionless on the hillside as if an artist had captured the scene in still life. Sea gulls called overhead as they glided and swooped toward silvery dunes for the night. Grasses rippled in the marshes, golden from the setting sun. In the quietness, it seemed we could hear laughter of children playing in the barn's hay mows, see the row of gingerbread cottages with their porches full of guests, hear the haunting music of the old melodeon accompanying Sunday twilight hymn sings. We talked of this day filled with fragrances, feelings, sounds and silences. With a sense of wonder, we had shared a beginning of New England history, a time of strong men and women sturdy in character. We felt a oneness with those who had a part in molding history, education and government.

We remembered that this same closeness was expressed by Benjamin Choate, great grandson of the first Choate settler on the island. When he moved to the mainland, he wrote in a family journal that "the thoughts of leaving the old place made the tears start." So it is with all who leave this spot.

Indeed, our day on the island will not be forgotten. We shared a communion with nature, a brush with history and fellowship with Choates, past and present. Even though Agnes will no longer make trips downriver with us, we shall experience many happy returns to the island she loved through her poetry and writings.

May this book be an invitation for you to listen to the island's call. Once you have been caught up in the hypnotic spell of a time and place set apart, you will return.

Today I Went to an Island

Today I went to an island…
    An island I used to know.
Fields and hilltop and pebbly shore
    Were the same as of years ago.

The old-time homestead on the knoll
    Still stood as in childhood days;
But silent and vacant the rooms inside
    Where only echo stays.

No voices calling through empty rooms
    As in that long-gone past
An island is a lonely spot
    To the one who goes there last.

Agnes Choate Wonson

BIBLIOGRAPHY

American Ancestry, Giving Name and Descent in the Male Line of Americans Whose Ancestors Settled in the U.S. Previous to the Declaration of Independence. V.5. Joel Munsell's Sons, 1968.

Bell, N. S., comp. *Pathways of the Puritans*. Framingham, Massachusetts Bay Colony Tercentenary Commission.

Boston Evening Transcript. Boston, June 28, 1930.

Brown, S. H. *Works of Rufus Choate with a Memoir of His Life*. Boston, Little Brown & Co., c. 1930.

Choate, Agnes. Diaries and journals.

Choate family guest book of Choate Island. 1877-1914.

Choate, Rufus. Illustrated private journal and diary 1874-1886.

Crawford, M. C. *Famous Families of Massachusetts*. Boston, Little, Brown & Co., c. 1930.

Crowell, R. *History of the Town of Essex*, 1634-1868. Springfield, Mass., Samuel Bowlles & Co., c. 1913.

Cutter. *Genealogical and Personal Memoirs Relating to the Families of Boston and Eastern Massachusetts*. N. Y., Lewis Historical Pub. Co., 1908.

Essex County Registry of Deeds. Salem, Massachusetts.

Essex Echo Newspaper. Essex, Mass., August 1889.

Essex Institute. *Vital Records of Essex, Massachusetts to the End of the Year 1849*. Salem, Mass., Essex Institute, 1908.

Felt, J. B. *History of Ipswich, Essex and Hamilton*. 1834.

Fuess, C. M. *Rufus Choate; the Wizard of the Law.* N.Y., Minton, Balch and Company, 1928.

Hurd, D. H. *History of Essex County, Massachusetts with Biographical Sketches of Many of its Prominent Men.* Philadelphia, J. W. Lewis, 1888.

Jameson, E. O. *The Choates in America.* Boston, Alfred Mudge & Sons Printers, 1896.

Martin, E. S. *Life of Joseph Hodges Choate.* V.I., N.Y., Scribner's Sons, 1920.

Probate Records. Salem, Massachusetts.

Townsend, C. W. *Sand Dunes and Salt Marshes.* Dana Estes & Company Publishers. 1913.

Waters, T. F. *Ipswich in the Massachusetts Bay Colony, 1633-1700.* Ipswich, Mass., Ipswich Historical Society, 1905.

AUTHOR—

MARY WONSON (1921-2022) was a native of Mississippi. Following graduation from college with a degree in Library Science, she worked as a librarian in Mississippi, Washington, D.C. and Massachusetts. In addition to hobbies of gardening, sewing, water color painting and music, she has pursued her interest in research by taking courses in non-fiction writing.

PHOTOGRAPHER—

ROGER WONSON, (1924-   ) an avid free-lance photographer, has studied at the Montserrat School of Visual Art and has taught photography at Gordon College. He was a Senior Engineer in electronics at Raytheon Company.

Combining their interest in music, art and photography, Mary and Roger have presented multi-media programs for historical, arts and craft societies. They have co-authored articles with photographs for the following publications: Musart, Modern Photography, Family Hanyman, Workbench, Electronics Progress, and the David C. Cook religious magazines. The Wonsons resided in Beverly, Mass., and are parents of three daughters.

POET—

AGNES CHOATE WONSON (1882-1981) attended Salem Normal School and studied art at Eric Pape School in Boston. Until her death in July, 1981 (approaching her 99th birthday) she was actively involved in submitting poetry and art work for publication. One collection of her poems, Candles of Memory, has been published. Agnes had a gift of portraying what she saw and felt with charm and sincerity, inspiring those who knew her through her creative work.

www.ingramcontent.com/pod-product-compliance
Lightning Source LLC
Chambersburg PA
CBHW061404160426
42811CB00100B/1458